Praise for From Thorns to Blossoms

"Heidi's book is so beautifully and honestly written. It is going to help so many people break free from their own personal trauma. I think it is an incredible resource, and I am just so proud of her!" **Ashley Willis**, Host of *The Naked Marriage Podcast*, Author of *The Counterfeit Climax*, Biblical Counselor

"Heid's recount of her own personal life and faith offers a memoir rich with practical wisdom to help others recognize and hear God's voice in their lives. Her experiences, marked by pain and eventually healing, serve as a testament to the power of faith and the possibility of transformation through divine grace. This is a must read!" **Eric & Kristen Kennedy,** *The Recovery Vow Podcast*

"From Thorns to Blossoms" is a powerful and inspiring account of Heidi's journey from childhood rejection and pain to healing and purpose through her faith in God. With raw honesty, she shares the wounds of rejection that shaped her early life and led her down destructive paths in search of love and acceptance. What makes this book truly inspiring is Heidi's unwavering faith and commitment to spiritual growth, even in her darkest moments. Her transformation from a hurt, insecure girl to a strong woman of faith is moving to witness. Her story serves as a powerful testimony to God's redeeming love and ability to bring beauty from ashes." **Vanessa Martindale,** bestselling author, speaker, and founder of Blended Kingdom Families and Co-Founder of SEVN Therapy Co.

FROM THORNS *to* BLOSSOMS

MY FORTY YEAR *journey* OF HOW GOD
HEALED MY *rejection* WOUNDS

HEIDI DRURY

This book is dedicated to my granddaughters Raylynn, Cadence, Emma, Kamma and Sophie. May you always know in your heart of hearts that God is your source for all things. Each of you was created on purpose for a purpose and I look forward to seeing how God uses your gifts and strengths to make this world a better place.

Table of Contents

ACKNOWLEDGEMENTS

There is no place I would rather start than to give God all the glory for helping me write this book. It goes way beyond that. Without God, Jesus and The Holy Spirit, I would not have the freedom I do today. There are no human words I can express for the gift of salvation, redemption and sanctification. He saved my life, my marriage, and broke family inequities that will impact my children and my children's children for generations to come.

To my husband, my Kenny in shining armor. Today that has a different meaning and weight. Your courage to allow God into all the nooks and crannies of your heart and soul, have created you into a husband I never believed could exist. Thank you for your willingness to surrender all of yourself to Gods leadership. Because you took that step of faith, I now have someone who makes me feel secure, heard, seen, cherished, desired and loved. I am so excited to continue our life's journey as a team on fire for God and grow His Kingdom purpose in our marriage.

To my children, all of you, the ones who I birthed and to the ones who came as a bonus gift, I cannot image life without you in it. Boys', being your mother has been the most rewarding, satisfying and challenging job I have ever had. Watching you both grow into men, find who you are and what you want to be, and start your own journeys into marriage and fatherhood gives me joy deep in my soul. I could not be more proud to call you my sons. Daughters', even though I did not grow you inside of my body, I cherish each of you for the special relationships we have developed over these years.

I pray as we get older and life continues to change, you know I will always be your biggest fan. Because of each of you, I am a MorMor, (grandmother in Swedish). These precious grandchildren are the best gift anyone has ever given me and I will be forever grateful.

Mom, life has not always been fun or easy, but you have always been one of my biggest supporters. Thank you for making so many sacrifices in your life so we could experience people and places that would not have been possible otherwise.

MMM and my entire adoptive family, the impact you have had in and on my life far transcends flesh and blood. Having siblings, bonus dads and moms, extra grandparents, aunts and uncles, sister-in-law's, brother-in-law's, cousins, nephews and nieces has helped in my healing journey to feel unconditionally loved and wanted. God knew I needed all of you. Thank you will never be a good enough word for all the ways you have and continue to pour into my life. I am eternally grateful.

Pastor Elijah Vogel, thank you for getting in the mud with us and pointing us back to God, His truth and His plan for our lives and marriage. To our small group family at Camino Community Church, we would not be where we are today without your love, support, guidance and faithfulness. Each of you has played a vital role in our healing journeys. Bob and Betsy Verzello, if it was not for you and Marriage 52 at Green Valley Church we would never have learned about Pastor Jimmy Evans and the *How We Love* book that was part of saving our lives and marriage. To all my friends, family and the leaders of Celebrate Recovery, thank you for showing me how to get the plank out of my own eye.

To our first friend in East Texas, Melinda Gibbs, thank you for stepping out of your comfort zone and inviting us to church. Leann and Charlie Morris, you have always made us feel welcomed and treated us like we have known you forever. Thank you LeAnn for the help, support, guidance and suggestions while writing and editing. To my other beta readers Claire Lewis and Melissa Antoine, I will always be grateful for your time and insight.

To the authors who I think of as part of our marriage restoration team: Dr. Henry Cloud and Dr. John Townsend of the *Boundaries* books, Kay and

Milan Yerkovich *How We Love,* Gary Thomas *Sacred Marriage,* Tim Keller *The Meaning of Marriage,* Les and Leslie Parrot, Dr. Emerson Eggerichs *Love and Respect,* Stephen Arterburn, Fred and Brenda Stoeker *Every Man's Battle and Every Heart restored,* John and Stasi Eldredge, Gary Chapman, Dr. Tony Evans *Kingdom Marriage,* Debra Fileta, Sue Johnson, Stephen and Holly Furtick, Phil and Jase Robertson, and last but not least Jimmy Evans *Marriage on The Rock, The Four Laws of Love, Vision Retreat,* and *The Strengths Based Marriage.*

A special thank you to XO Marriage, Jimmy and Karen Evans, Brent Evans, Eric Gomez, Theresa Tomas, Pam Southers, Daniel Van, Maria Hazzard, our marriage mediator team, all of the XO staff, board members and donors who make it possible to keep XO creating content that saves marriages and families just like mine.

Thank you to Jenny Morgan for your wisdom, time and encouragement during the editing process.

A very special shout out to my longest relationship, my ride-or-die, my bestie of besties, Kelly Hull. No matter how far away we are, or how much time passes between hellos or visits, I have always been able to count on you. You have never judged my stupid decisions or made me feel less than for my life choices. Many of my best memories include you and I wouldn't want it any other way. I look forward to growing old with you in my life.

INTRODUCTION

Have you ever read Exodus in the Bible and thought to yourself how unyielding and stubborn those Israelites were. Why would they ever want to go back to a place they were slaves? Why did it take them so long to believe God loved and cherished them so much and recognize He wanted to bless them beyond comprehension? Who would ever choose to live in disobedience like the Israelites for forty years? Me, that's who.

Just like them, I spent a total of forty years of my life allowing the pain of rejection I experienced in childhood to influence my choices. I wanted to feel accepted, loved, wanted, cherished, secure, and safe. The problem was that I looked to all the wrong people and things to tell me who I was and if I was acceptable. And because I did, I was always left feeling more rejected, shameful, unlovable, alone, scared, anxious, insecure, defective, empty, and desperate than the time before.

In my story, you will read about the main characters in my dysfunctional family, including the abuse I experienced at the hands of a male cousin. I will show how I started searching for acceptance at a young age by looking for love in all the wrong places and how that led me to compromise my values and beliefs. You will discover how I thought being married and a mother would solve all my problems. You will read how my family dynamics and inequities influenced my relational patterns and life-altering decisions. I expose you to all of my raw, gritty, sinful choices and to the consequences that followed.

I desire that after reading my book, you do not waste one more day believing the lies that you are unlovable and not good enough. On these pages, you will see someone who has been through many of your experiences—a woman who can relate to your deep pain. You will see the freedom I now walk in, and the chains I no longer carry are available to you, too. If God can forgive me and cleanse me from all the awful, immoral things I did, then He absolutely can do it for you, too. I pray that my vulnerability reassures you, "If we confess our sins, he is faithful and righteous to forgive us our sins and to cleanse us from *ALL* unrighteousness."(1 John 1:9 Emphases added).

If you are ready to learn how I found true freedom from my past wounds, hurts, and choices, and you want the same for your life, I invite you to keep reading.

SECTION 1

MY FRACTURED FAMILY

"Woe to the world because of offenses. For offenses will inevitably come, but woe to that person by whom the offense comes."

Matthew 18:7 (CSB)

CHAPTER 1

Where The Rejection Wounds Started

M ost of what I know about my biological father is not from the time we spent together creating memories or life experiences. It comes from what other people in my life have told me. Mainly my mom and his dad, my grandpa. I heard things like he was an alcoholic or that he was a mechanic in the navy and won my mother's wedding ring in a poker game and that he was often abusive to my mother. I learned he was mad and blamed my mother that I was not a boy. Another thing I heard was that right after I was born, he brought his mistress over to see me. Other than that, I never knew him or about him. I never learned what his favorite color was or if he was a Chevy or Ford guy. Did he like to read the comic strips from the Sunday newspaper? After working all day, would he want to sit in a recliner or on the couch? What was his go to meal? Did he like vanilla, strawberry, or chocolate ice cream?

I know we spent time together and did things, because I have the Kodak pictures to prove it. There are a few events I can recall doing with him, but I don't know if those are actual memories or the stories talked about while looking at those pictures. We lived in California, and my dad often took us to the Oakland Zoo. I can almost smell old sardines and hear the barking seals when I think about those outings. I can see myself standing on the outer rim of the enclosure with my face pressed against the small, round window, waiting to steal a glimpse of a seal as it swam past. A trip to the zoo also meant I would eat one of my most cherished treats: a rectangle-shaped pink popcorn.

I can recall spending time with my dad at a horse park. After we got out of the car, we would walk to a small A-frame shed where he paid for tickets to ride the horses. As my sister and I stood in line, we would hang on the white fence, arms crossed, leaning out as our heads followed the horses and riders around the large, oval course. I loved the white horses with the large brown spots, like the one from the popular show, "The Lone Ranger." In many ways, it was like a merry-go-round. When the ride was over, the horses stopped, and an attendant helped us on and off the horses. I am trying to remember if we were allowed to ask for a particular horse or if we had to take whichever was next in line.

When we had shorter visits with Dad, we went to eat at Samboos or IHOP. It was always for breakfast—never dinner—and he usually ordered a Denver omelet. Those looked so weird to me, and I didn't understand why someone would eat eggs with all those strange, colored dots on them. My sister and I would sit together in the booth facing our dad. She would order pigs in a blanket, and I always had French toast.

When I remember the times spent with my grandparents and my dad, I think of the things I did or the presents I received—not life lessons I learned or conversations we had. There was no time for snuggling on the couch or watching cartoons while curled up in Dad's lap. I have no memory of him (or anyone else in his family) offering me comfort in any way, shape, or form. Did I ever get a boo-boo or an ouchie? Did my sister or cousin ever pull my hair or steal a toy from my hands? Did I ever trip on the concrete and skin my knee or elbow? Was I ever sick with a sore throat or tummy ache? There had to be times when I needed one of those relatives, especially my dad, to run to me and tell me that I was okay, that I mattered, or that the pain would stop soon. There must have been.

When I was in first grade, my dad's mom died in her sleep due to complications from liver cancer. I cried when my mom sat me down and told me the news. Then, I blamed my mom because I believed it was her fault. I was mad at her for days. Even though this was my first experience with death, I somehow knew that dying meant I would never see Grandma again.

It was about this time my dad's visits, trips, calls, presents, and any time alone started to wane. Over the next few months, he would show up less and less until the visits stopped. When it was his weekend to visit, my mom would get us ready by fixing our hair and helping us put on our best Sunday dresses and shoes. She would allow us to sit in the big window of our downstairs apartment. Facing the street, we waited with our little faces pressed against the glass, anticipating Dad's turn into our driveway. But there were many times that he didn't show up. After what seemed like hours, Mom would make up an excuse for his absence. There was so much confusion in our little hearts, and tears ran down our cheeks as Mom convinced us to leave our spots at the window. She would try to cheer us up by being funny or get us to stop crying by taking us to Moo's Ice Cream.

As visits with my father grew less and less, so did time with my grandfather, uncles, aunts, and cousins. Before they completely disappeared, I overheard some grown-ups talk about my dad. They would try to figure out where he was, where he was working, and where he was living. Why was he not paying child support to my mom? It was as if he fell off the face of the earth and vanished into thin air. My grandfather took trips all over California looking for my dad, but he never returned with the answer I longed for.

When I was about 9 years old, I saw my dad out of the blue. My mom, sister and I were in the car heading from the store to my other grandma's house. A few blocks away from our destination, we spotted my dad standing outside next to a car. He watched as we drove by. Our heads twisted to look at him as long as we could. Through tears, I begged my mom to tell me why my dad was there. Could we turn around and see him? Why was he so close and not coming to see us? In that moment, I believed I was not as important or special to him as whatever else he was doing. I needed to be better, smarter, and prettier. I must have done something so wrong. Why else would a father not want to see his child? It had to be my fault. I told myself I didn't deserve to have him or any other man as my father.

Growing up I would create stories in my mind about where my dad lived, what kind of job he had, whom he was married to, what car he drove, and why he wasn't around. I was sure I had other siblings I had never met. I dreamed that one day, I would have enough money to hire a private detective who could tell me all the details I had long imagined. This person would fill in all my blanks.

One spring day, when I was 34, my mom called me with news from my biological dad's sister. She had told my mother that my father had passed away. My mom shared the details with me, but after I heard that my father was dead, I couldn't hear anything else. I was in shock. I hung up the phone and continued my chores as if nothing had happened. My youngest son was in my arms as I took the laundry from the wash, opened the laundry room door, walked to the clothesline, and hung up the wet clothes. With my baby at my feet and a clothespin in hand, a rush of emotions took me by surprise as I reached down to grab the next towel. I dropped to my knees and sobbed out loud. My husband came from the house because he heard my cries. He asked me what was wrong, and I could barely find the words to tell him about my phone call. My husband was confused by my severe reaction because he knew how I felt about my dad (or what he thought I felt about him). As I tried to stand up and find my voice, the 7-year-old Heidi wailed out, "Now I will never get the chance to have a relationship with him. He will never know my children, meet you, or see what I have done with my life. Any chance for him to get his head out of his butt, walk down our driveway, grab me, hold me in his arms, and tell me he is sorry for leaving me is gone. I will never hear him tell me he loves me." I felt abandoned and rejected by my earthly father forever.

CHAPTER 2

I Had To Be The Strong One

As far back as I can remember, the places I called home while I was growing up included just three people:

1. Me

2. My sister, Sarah

3. My mom, Jane

There was never a man of the house, a dad, a stepdad, a live-in boyfriend, or even a brother under our four walls. I'm not sure if this was intentional on my mom's part after she and my dad divorced or if that is just how it worked out. There was only one real boyfriend that I can recall. His name was Donald. He had red hair and a bushy red beard, and to this day, I can picture him standing in front of me in either a bright flannel shirt or a shirt with crazy prints all over it.

My sister and I liked Donald. He was kind and gentle with us. When I think of him, my mind brings me to Disneyland. I could not have been more than four years old, but I know he and Mom took us there to celebrate Sarah's birthday before she went to kindergarten. That trip has stuck with me my entire life. I can bring forward highlights of that adventure that I have stored in my memory: The Haunted Mansion, Riverboat Cruise, It's A

Small World, Thunder Mountain, and the abominable snowman from the Matterhorn ride. Of course, Disneyland is a magical place, and it is hard to forget your first time there. But this was not just about the place we visited but more about how the four of us looked and sounded like and felt like a real family—something I never, ever had with my biological dad, mother, and sister. I believed this was my new family, and I *really* wanted it to last forever. But it didn't.

When Mom and Donald eventually broke up, my 4 or 5-year-old dreams, hopes, and desires of having a "real" family went down the drain. But I wasn't the only one heartbroken. The breakup devastated my mom. You may wonder how I can remember that time and how it affected my mom. Well, as far back as I can recall, she never kept anything from us, especially her emotions and feelings.

Mom has always been an open book, though perhaps too open sometimes. She is very forthcoming in talking to me about everything and anything when it suits her. As a child, I just thought we were close. Wasn't this how all moms and daughters talked to each other? Mom shared her feelings and beliefs about my biological dad, my grandma, my aunt and uncle, people from her work, friends, neighbors, and even my sister. She would tell me when she was short on funds, couldn't pay a bill, and had to borrow money. If she was overwhelmed or burdened or suffering from depression, I knew about it.

The problem with this intense level of sharing was that the knowledge became a burden on my little shoulders. I worried about my mom a lot. I felt responsible for how she was feeling, and because I did not want to burden her further, I played the role of the strong child. I could handle anything thrown at me, or so I pretended. I was too afraid to speak up. I did not want her to have any more worries, pressures, or things that upset her. I did not want to make her life any more complicated. The problem was I did not have the tools to help her. I did not have a way to make money to help pay the bills. I could not give her ideas about communicating better with Grandma Lucy. I was not a counselor or a doctor, so I couldn't treat her depression or help "fix" my sister's medical problems.

Mom's transparency was the reason I knew how she felt about the breakup with Donald. She treated me like I was her best girlfriend, and she told me that the reason Donald didn't want to marry her was because he did not want to be a father. He didn't want the responsibility of raising two small girls. *Oh, so it was my and my sister's fault he left!* Those were not the exact words Mom said, but that is what five-year-old me believed. *Great, another "Daddy" rejected me because I was not good enough in some way.*

I did not believe I could go to my mom with my problems and issues. Sure, she would usually hear me out and listen and give comfort when I needed it, but that was more to ease her anxiety than to hear me, see me, or truly understand what I was going through. Many times, her comfort felt like a means to an end. Her goal was to get me better as fast as possible because if she couldn't, that made her a bad mom. I believed my pain made life worse for her.

As "friends" (not as a mother and her two young daughters), there were so many times the three of us had a blast together. We would often get in the car and go on day-trip adventures. Mom would tell us beforehand, "We have this amount of money for the day, and we can go this far." We would load up the car with essentials, like Tab Cola, cheese, salami, crackers, Jolly Ranchers, extra clothes, blankets, books, and maybe a Barbie or two. KFRC was always playing 70's music on the radio, and when the comedic Doctor Don Rhodes came on, we would quiet down to see what weird, crazy thing he had to say.

One of the places we loved going the most was San Francisco, where we would go to the zoo and the Exploratorium. In Golden Gate Park, we went to the California Academy of Science, watched the star show at the Planetarium, and shopped in Union Square. In Oakland, there was Fairyland, Jack London Square, the zoo, and Fenton's Ice Cream. If we ended up in Berkeley, we would stop at the Lawrence Hall of Science or walk around the university campus. We would travel up and down the coast, play on the beaches, and visit the state parks.

Mom was very creative in looking for discount coupons or special free days to get into some of these attractions. I know she sacrificed a lot of things for herself to make us happy and provide for us. She often went without new clothes and drove cars that broke down, and our house didn't have new furniture or fancy paintings on the walls. Mom was the sole provider and breadwinner, which was rough on her and us. My dad had stopped contributing financially way before he disappeared from our lives, and we often had to rely on food stamps and help from the state to make ends meet. I knew we didn't have a lot, but I never really felt poor, at least not when we were little.

Mom believed that moving from Richmond to Napa would be the best thing for all of us, especially my sister and me. We left shortly after my dad's mom died, around the time my dad stopped coming around. Those were the worst days of my young life. I had to leave the only house I had ever known and all my best friends, and we moved over an hour away from our extended family. We moved in July so that Sarah and I could settle before school started. I remember lying in my bed in my new room, crying and being so mad at my mom. I was sure she had ruined my life, and I was afraid I would never make any new friends.

Mom promised to do everything she could to ensure we stayed in touch with our friends from our hometown. She told us we could call whenever we wanted to, have sleepovers, and visit them as often as possible. I am not sure this ever happened. I cannot bring to mind any of those friends ever coming to Napa to stay the weekend with us. That summer, I felt so alone, rejected, and empty, even though we were the ones who left. I concluded that the reason I never saw or heard from those friends again was because something was wrong with me. I must have done something bad, and their parents didn't like me, or worse yet, my friends felt that way. Other than the crying, I internalized the grief. I had to keep up the front and be strong as not to cause Mom any more heartache.

The move was hard on all three of us. Despite Mom's best efforts, we knew she was struggling. Some days she would not get dressed, leave the couch, or even get out of bed. She had this thin, mint-green robe and a pink scarf she wore around her head for days on end. Often, we heard her sobbing from her room. I was scared she was sick or dying. At the time, I had no idea she felt depressed and isolated.

Sarah and I played outside for hours to avoid waking Mom up. I created a little house in a storage garage in the back of our main house. Along the entire back wall was a plywood shelf. I had blankets and pillows, chairs, lots of books, and art supplies for coloring and drawing set up there. I spent hours reading and pretending to be a teacher to my older sister. I made sheets of math problems and lists of things Sarah had to do (like collecting worms and snails) to consider her "classwork" complete for the day. We played tetherball, swept our "house," rode bikes around the neighborhood, and picked weeds from the front lawn.

Eventually, Grandma Lucy (my mom's mother) and her sister (my Great-Aunt Anna) had to come to Napa and "whip" my mom into shape. They took my sister and me back to their house in Richmond to give my mom a few days to get herself together. I don't know what Mom did during our away days, but when we returned, she was better, at least for a while.

The best way to explain living with Mom was like riding the old-fashioned wooden roller coasters. In the good seasons, up, up, up we went. Those days were filled with laughter, music, and adventures. There was peace in our lives and in our home. But we knew not to get too comfortable because what went up must come down. Soon we would be hanging on for dear life as everything came crashing down. We knew Mom was in one of her "bad" times when we were whisked away to Grandma Lucy's house or moved around like chess pieces to whomever wanted to take us in for a few days while Mom had some rest time.

We bounced around a lot over the years. As a child, I thought visiting all these places and people was so cool. But over time, I slowly began to feel like I did not matter to her or that other things and people were more important to her than my sister and me. I had no clue how hard raising us on her own was and what a toll it took on her mentally, physically, and financially. All I knew as a child was that I wanted to be with my mom, where I felt I was supposed to be. And when I couldn't be with her, I felt confused, worthless and abandoned.

Over the years, our relationship continued to be up and down, good and bad, close and distant. Now that I'm an adult, some of Mom's moods and emotions are easier for me to navigate, though others still leave me feeling hurt and confused. Yes, I know my mother loves me in the way she knows how. But that doesn't mean there aren't times I mourn deep inside for her to be the mother I always wanted and needed her to be.

CHAPTER 3

All Of Moms Attention

Work and depression were not the only things that kept my mom away. My sister, Sarah, was born with a birth defect: she was missing one of her C-spine. When she was learning to sit up, they noticed she would cry and cry, and not much would soothe her. She also had trouble holding up her head. After Sarah's diagnosis, she had her first surgery before she ever walked. She was in a full body cast from her belly to over her head. Only her little face showed through. My sister learned to crawl and walk while wearing that body cast

I think one of her extensive surgeries was when I was four or five years old. Sarah was a patient at Children's Hospital in Oakland. I stayed with Grandma Lucy and Aunt Anna so my mom could be at the hospital with my sister. They took me to the hospital the day of (or maybe the day after the surgery) so they could visit her. I remember the sterile, antiseptic smells of the large, cold waiting room and sitting in a blue plastic chair as we all waited for news about how Sarah was doing.

A nurse or volunteer took me into the "I'm waiting on a sibling playroom," so all the adults could visit my sister. I was not allowed to go back to see her because I was too young. I didn't want to go with this stranger; I wanted to see my mom and sister! I was scared Sarah might die or that my mom was going to stay in the hospital forever with her, which would mean I would have to go live with Grandma Lucy. I loved my grandma, but I wanted my mom. This playroom had coloring pages, games, art supplies, dolls, blocks, and all the cool toys of the early 1970s. The supervising adult sat down with me, and I pretended the doll had a broken arm. I made a cast using some actual hospital bandages to wrap her up.

Throughout our childhood, Sarah was in and out of doctors' offices and hospitals for one thing or another: bone issues, epilepsy, depression, and other psychological disorders. It isn't always easy, convenient, or permissible to bring along a second child when you are trying to deal with the medical ailments of another. For this reason, I was bounced around to different relatives and people. Since my father was not available, my mom did not have much choice but to find other people to help her out while she was getting treatment for my sister.

My sister and I were so close growing up. We are only 15 months apart, and we were all each other had. We played together as many siblings do, but it was much more than that because we were best friends. Other than the time Sarah was in the hospital, we never spent a night apart until late into adolescence. She was my safety blanket, and I was hers.

Our relationship started to change as we grew older, went out into the world, and built friendships apart from each other. When Sarah went into junior high, she attended a Christian school, and I went to a public school. Everyone thought it would be better for Sarah to be protected on a smaller campus with kids who would better understand her health issues. (Sadly, that was not the case. Even Christian kids can still be mean).

As Sarah's body changed, she stopped growing up and started filling out. She had inherited the "bigger bones" from our dad's mother's side. The truth is Sarah was overweight—not obese but larger than most teenage girls want to be. Her friends started getting taller while she was getting wider, and that caused a divide between them. Her weight was a divide for us too. The taller I grew, the leaner I became. I shot up almost seven inches between seventh and eighth grade. I looked like a bean pole. If you are the older sister to a string bean and you look more like an apple, guess who becomes jealous of how their sister looks? Sarah used to say she could look at a grape and gain weight, but I could eat a whole pizza and not gain an ounce.

Sarah also believed nothing terrible ever happened to me—she thought she had all the health issues and all the problems. We never talked about my problems because I was the "strong" one. I was not supposed to have problems, and if I did, I had to keep them to myself. I had to pretend that I was okay so as not to upset my mother or cause her any more pain. Sarah did not know how much her health issues impacted me. My mom attended every one of my sister's softball practices, games, and events. Everything Sarah did, my mom was there to witness it. I was often left to do all my special things alone or with a friend. I blamed Sarah for this because she got all of Mom's attention. I can remember Mom telling me, "Your sister needs me more than you do. You are strong and can handle it. Sarah can't." My sister and I both resented and envied each other, but we never knew each other's pain because we never talked about it.

As the years went on, Sarah's mental illness became more challenging and time-consuming to manage and treat. In high school, she had a few friends she had known since we moved to Napa. They stuck by her side despite her mood swings and lengthy absences from classes. She was so introverted and shy, and she seemed to prefer being alone than with people. Like Mom, the significant differences in Sarah's moods and how she handled life were pretty severe. For months she would be on top of the world, trying new things, playing sports, hanging out with friends, going to football games and dances, and doing all the typical teenage things. She laughed a lot and seemed happy. But then it was as if a switch flipped, and Sarah became someone totally different. She would give away many of her prized possessions and refuse to leave the house. She would quit her job if she had one, not call friends back, and not shower or change clothes for days. Sarah had severe, angry outbursts during which she would throw things at Mom and me, many times breaking those items or damaging walls in the house. We all feared she was suicidal. You can guess how this made Mom want to hover over Sarah and care for her like a wounded bird. She would attend to every beck and call Sarah had and even ones Sarah never asked for. All of these things were an attempt to make Sarah "snap out of it."

After she graduated high school, my sister went to live with Grandma Lucy. Jumping from job to job, Sarah had difficulty deciding who she wanted to be and what career path she wanted to study for. No matter what anyone said or did for Sarah, she continued her emotional pattern of good and then bad, followed by some more good and some more bad. Soon, the bad times and seasons were longer than the good ones.

One day, when she was about 20 or 21, Sarah woke up, gave away most of her belongings, packed a small bag, hopped on a bus, and rode out of our lives. Last any of us know, she was living and working in Seattle, Washington. She touched base a few times with my mom, Grandma Lucy, and sometimes me until 2006. After that, she emailed my mom and told her to get lost, leave her alone, and not contact her any further.

Over the years, I continued to stuff my resentments and hatred of the things my sister did to my family and me. I lived life as if she was dead. I told myself this was what I had to do to protect myself. Deep down, I was so sad because I missed her like crazy. We have not spent much time together or talked since I was in my early 20s, so I probably wouldn't recognize Sarah if I passed her on the street or heard her voice. I have no idea if her hair is still super thick and blonde or if she is now gray. I have no idea if her skin still looks like a porcelain doll with beautiful pink cheeks. Has she ever been married? Does she have any children of her own? Is her favorite color still blue? Does she still love pigs in a blanket and French dip sandwiches? Is she still alive?

CHAPTER 4

Two Grandmas In One House

My sister and I spent a lot of time with Grandma Lucy (my mom's mom), especially in our younger years. When I think back, she and her sister, Anna, are in most of my memories. Aunt Anna lived with Grandma Lucy because way before I came around, Grandpa Eric (my mom's dad) died. Having never married, Anna moved in and was there until the day she died.

I loved Grandma Lucy wholeheartedly, but ours wasn't always an easy relationship. I didn't always believe she loved me like she loved my cousins and especially my sister, Sarah. No matter what I did or how accomplished I tried to become, it never felt like enough for her. It wasn't like she would withhold affection or love from me, but many of her actions made me think she didn't love me.

I vividly remember one time Grandma Lucy bought my sister a pack of underwear. There was a pair for each day of the week, and each had a different character on them with a different color lace around the legs and waistband. She handed them to my sister in front of me. My sister held them up, but because they were not her size, she said to Grandma Lucy, "Give them to

Heidi" and handed me the pack. Well, Grandma Lucy took them from my hand and said, "I'll see if Chloe wants them." (Chloe is my female cousin.)

Then there was the time I asked for the *Little House on The Prairie* book collection for Christmas. The whole family got together on Christmas Eve to eat and hand out gifts. As we were opening presents, guess what Chloe received from Grandma Lucy? The entire box set of the exact books I wanted. I was devastated, and to this day, I have no recollection of what I got instead. Of course, Chloe may have wanted those books too, but why could our grandma not have given both of us a set of books?

It baffles my adult brain how moments like those had so much power to create lasting beliefs, especially when Grandma Lucy and I shared so many extraordinary times together. She was always there when my mom could not be the mom she should have been. We stayed with Grandma Lucy and Aunt Anna so often that I was sure we lived there. I learned to ride a bike in front of her house and pick myself up off the ground while learning to roller skate over the cracks that tripped me on the sidewalk. Even in kindergarten, I walked to her house after school instead of our apartment. We spent many Halloweens trick-or-treating in her neighborhood, even after we moved to Napa. All the major holidays and family birthdays were celebrated at her house.

Grandma Lucy taught me how to sew, cook, and clean. She lavished special trips on us, like when she drove us to Disneyland or flew us to Minnesota for Christmas when I was eight. Every year until I graduated high school, she took Sarah and me shopping for clothes. She made us special matching dresses and nightgowns each year, and every costume I wore for theatre productions, every skirt for ballet and dance recitals, and every skating outfit for practice and competitions was made by Grandma Lucy.

Even though I thought she loved me less than the others, Grandma Lucy's house was a source of comfort and joy for me. I would spend hours curled up on the hideous brown-flower couch when I was sick. She would wrap me in one of her handmade quilts and soothe my sore throat with a hot cherry Jell-O mix or a lemon, honey, and sugar concoction. Grandma Lucy knew I loved spaghetti, so she would make it for me whenever I was there. The best part was she had these white plastic bibs with a thin red trim and tie.

On the bib was a guy eating spaghetti while wearing a bib with a guy eating spaghetti, and so on. I remember thinking those were so cool, and I refused to eat spaghetti unless I could wear the bib.

At Grandma Lucy's house, I was interested in everything I thought was old. I was curious about all the family antiques passed down from generation to generation. She would sit with me and explain the origin stories of all the knickknacks. She wanted me to know who my family was through those things. Today, many of her teacups, vases, bowls, silverware, candlestick holders, plates, jewelry, and pictures sit on my shelves and hang on my walls as reminders of Grandma Lucy and our times together.

Grandma Lucy lived just shy of her 101st birthday. Her mind was sharp as a tack up until that day. She was sure it was because she had done the *New York Times* crossword puzzle daily. Her hands were rattled with arthritis, but she refused to let that stop her from knitting or holding a deck of cards. We developed a closer relationship in her last years, months, and days. She and I loved to go out for lunch after a day of clothes shopping, just like we had since I was five years old.

Since Anna lived with Lucy, it felt like I had two grandmas residing under the same roof. Anna was so cool. She started her adult life in the Midwest as a teacher, and before I started school, she retired from working at the naval yard in Oakland. Anna was tall and thin and had curly short brown hair. Her clothes seemed spectacular to me, and I often rummaged through her closet, trying on her dresses, scarves, and hats. She even had a genuine alligator purse. In her spare time, Anna loved to travel all over the world. She always sent us postcards from her stops and brought back really cool, exotic things from faraway locations. We would spend hours discussing these places while looking through stacks of Kodak pictures.

Growing up, I often wondered if Anna wasn't my real grandma. I had told myself that she was my mom's mom instead of Grandma Lucy. I am sure I conjured up this fantasy because I didn't feel loved by Grandma Lucy to the same degree as the others. So because Anna never married, I made up a crazy scenario in my mind where her lover was killed in World War II and she was pregnant with my mom at the time. Anna moved in with Grandma Lucy (and Grandpa Eric), gave birth to my mom, and Grandma Lucy raised her as her own. After all, things were different back then, and for a woman to be pregnant out of wedlock was scandalous. To protect her reputation and the baby, she pretended to be my mom's aunt and not her mother. I loved Anna so much and wanted her to be my grandma so badly.

I forget how old Anna was when she died, but I will never forget how old I was. It was November of 1987, and I was 17 years old. Her death devastated me, and I was torn up that she would not be at my graduation. She would never see me graduate from college, and she would never meet my husband when I married or my children if I had any. I think one of the hardest things I have ever done in my life was holding her hand as she lay rattled with broken bones from leukemia. I told her how much I loved her and how much she meant to me. I thanked her for loving me. I sure miss her.

CHAPTER 5

Family Isn't Always Safe

Four other people in my biological family significantly affected me growing up:

1. My mom's brother, Uncle Joe

2. Uncle Joe's wife, Aunt Stephanie

3. Joe and Stephanie's son, Brian-he was 6 years older than me

4. Joe and Stephanie's daughter, Chloe-she was 1 year younger than me

Joe and Stephanie's house was one of the places I spent a lot of time in my younger life, especially when Mom was having her hard seasons. My uncle kept to himself, and I don't think I spoke more than one hundred words to him my entire life. He had some chronic health issues that made it hard to understand what he was saying when he talked.

I believed my aunt was fake, like a plastic doll or some made-up character from TV. She was always dressed her best with her hair and makeup done, topped off with bracelets, earrings, and other jewelry. When she talked, I was sure she wasn't using her natural voice but was trying to give herself some fancy accent, like she was a royal family member. Neither Joe nor Stephanie was around much when I was sent to spend time at their house. I don't remember being supervised or disciplined or anyone cooking us food or telling us when we had to wake up or go to bed.

My relationship with Chloe was always super competitive. She is brilliant, and she got her Ph.D. in microbiology from Stanford University. I was jealous of her growing up. She had everything I thought I wanted: a mom and dad who were married, a big house with a pool, all the fun clothes from the best stores, all the latest and most fabulous toys, gadgets, and widgets, and when she was 16, her own classic sports car. We were always trying to one-up each other in just about everything we did. If I was in Algebra, she was in Algebra two. If I got new clothes, she got name-brand ones. If I got a pet, she got two. If I got a new comforter for my bed, she would have a new room and an incredible antique daybed. She even had a pen pal from Australia.

When I was in third grade, Chloe asked me if I wanted to miss school. She assured me of a way to miss it for weeks. Of course, I wanted to know how. I followed her outside, where she handed me a leaf and instructed me to rub it all over my body. Over the next few days, I broke out in a rash from head to toe. You guessed it: the leaf was poison oak. It turns out I am super allergic, so I swelled up like a purple Oompa Loompa from Willey Wonka, and just like Chloe said, I missed weeks of school.

I do not remember the exact age I was when my cousin Brian started molesting me, but I know it was before I started kindergarten. My first memory was Brian, Chloe, and I all in the shower together, maybe after having been in the pool or at the end of the night to get cleaned up before bed. I can distinctly remember Chloe being the one to tell me about what they did when they bathed together. They asked me if I wanted to do it with them. I was not sure what I thought was going to happen or what I was saying yes to, but that was the day it started: touching, fondling, caressing, and manipulating. There was never any penetration or oral; we only ever used our hands. Brian and Chloe never held a gun to my head or threatened to kill me if I ever told anyone. I wasn't dragged into it kicking and screaming or fighting to get away. I thought this was normal and that all cousins had secrets like ours, even though deep down I knew something was wrong with what was happening.

We didn't always sneak away to have our "private" time every time I visited. There are significant gaps in my memory of how often it took place or where it happened. The more concrete recollections bring me back to after they moved to their new home in El Sobrante. The house was two stories, and my aunt and uncle turned the downstairs into a game room. They had a TV, VCR, pinball machine, Ping-Pong table, and a pool table. We would drape blankets over the pool table and make a hideout. Sometimes, our "secrete" time was all three of us, and sometimes it was just Brian and me.

Brain also had a remote fort at the bottom of their property. When he invited me to play in his hideout, I knew what that meant. This was where I was exposed to porn for the first time. He kept magazines down there. Some were stacked in piles, others were open to specific pages, and some were ripped out, lining the floor. Girls, women, and men were on these pages doing things with their bodies I had never seen before. My young brain and delicate little girl eyes were exposed to images that would become pushed into the cracks of my subconscious. I was always confused but at the same time curious to understand what I saw. I knew these pictures were considered dirty, and it felt like I was seeing something I was not supposed to see. I knew that if my mom found out, I would be in big trouble.

I remember trying hard not to look or glance at them. I would gaze at the blue sky with fluffy white clouds or turn to the surrounding green trees, bushes, and plants. One plant appeared everywhere I turned my head: the fern. The leaves were one shade of green on top and another on the underside. I would focus so hard I could make out the small black dots on the underbelly of the leaves. As the leaves wilted from their weight and dropped down towards the damp brown dirt, I could imagine I was one of the little black dots hiding from my cousin. I would have been small, hidden by the protective drape of the leaves as it curved toward the earth. If I were there, I would be safe.

When I was 10 years old, the molesting stopped when my aunt, an officer in the juvenile detention system, found Brian and me with our pants down under the pool table. She took us each aside and questioned us. My most prominent memory of that day was when she said, "We do not have to tell anyone else; this can be our little secret."

Well, that is what happened. From that day forward, no one mentioned it again. I would see and spend time with them at Christmas, birthdays, etc., and we all acted like this was never an issue, problem, or something that should have been addressed or sought professional help for. My aunt swept it under the rug, and I did the same.

Once I started having my own family, there was little to no contact with my uncle, aunt or cousins. My uncle passed away when I was in my early 30s, but I had not seen him or my aunt since mid-1996. Chloe went on to become a prominent microbiologist in the Bay Area of California. She got married and has two children of her own whom I have never met. By God's grace, I never spent any time with Brian after my very early 20s. His story is not mine to tell, but I did hear from my mother that he passed away.

CHAPTER 6

My Bonus Family

I met my "adoptive" father at First Christian Church in Napa. I had just turned 10 years old, and our church was holding a father-daughter breakfast. If you did not have a father, you could register to be matched with a man for the day. So my mom signed me up. She hoped I would grow a relationship with a Christian man and his family who could fill a void in my life. When the day for the event arrived, I wore my best Sunday dress and my favorite sandals, and I had my hair all combed. My mom drove me to the church, and I met my new "dad," Charles Windsor. We sat at a table and talked as we ate. I learned he was married to Diana, and they had had their first child, a daughter named Scarlet, a few weeks earlier.

After this breakfast, our relationship continued to grow. I was accepted into Charles's little family, and I met extended family members like cousins, aunts, uncles, and grandparents. Many times, these people felt more like family than my real ones did. Their home, which was only about a mile away from my house, was one of the places my mom would send me when she was working, had things to handle with my sister, or could not take life in general.

The Windsor's let me tag along on fishing, camping, and skiing trips. Diana taught me how to bake family treats and further helped me learn to sew. My new-to-me dad even became my running coach. He would come home from working at Mare Island in Vallejo and take me around the neighborhood, teaching me breathing techniques, how to land my stride, and how to pace myself. On these runs, he would talk to me about life in general. The time we spent together as we ran felt special, and I believed we were the only two people in the world. I hung on to every word he said. As they left his mouth and went into my ears, they went down to my lungs and heart and filled me with life.

Three years after we first met, Charles and Diana had another child. This time, it was a boy named William. I now had a baby brother, but the excitement of his birth wore off quickly because his parents sat me down and told me that Charles had taken a job in a new city over eight hours away. This meant they had to move. The news destroyed me, and I didn't understand why I couldn't go with them or why he wouldn't have refused the job and stayed with me in Napa. I was afraid if they moved, I would never see them again. I believed this was another dad choosing something or someone other than me. I was sure it was my fault they were moving, which added to my belief that I was not lovable or good enough.

There were promises made about me flying down to see them and being able to connect when Charles was up in our area for work. I had one trip down there over Spring Break when I was 14, but he never came to see me when he was back in Napa. After that, the letters slowed down, and the calls became few and far between until we lost contact altogether. So many birthdays, holidays, and special events were lost over those absentee years. So much time was missing where I could have used their parental leadership and guidance.

The next time I spoke with or saw them, I was 23, Scarlett was 13, and William was 10. The Windsor's had moved back into the area, and I could not wait to see them all. The drive down to see them was mixed with excitement, anxious anticipation, and an expectation of what this would mean for us moving forward. Would this last? Would we see each other or talk regularly? Would we pick up where we left off? What had they been up to all these years? Did they miss me and wonder what life had been like for me?

The minute I saw Scarlett running from her house to greet me, it was as if time had never passed. The rest of the Windsor's joined us on the lawn.

We embraced and cried, squealed with excitement, hugged some more, and finally made our way into the house. We sat for hours and filled in all the gaps. After what seemed like only minutes, I had to be on my way back to where I lived.

Not long after our reunion, the Windsor's brought another girl, Rachel, into their home who lived down the street. Her family was very toxic and often abusive. Rachel was rough around the edges. She had never learned to eat properly and her table manners were non-existent. She was often too loud at the wrong time. Her clothes and hair were often a mess. But these bad habits and bumpy edges made all of us fall in love with her. Rachel was like a butterfly transforming before our eyes. The edges began to soften, and she grew into a beautiful, Jesus-loving ray of light in a dark world. She had these little sayings, ideas, and ways about her that made people stop and say, "What?" Rachel was quirky, silly, and sometimes off the wall, but at all times 100 percent herself.

Early one spring morning in 2005, she was tragically gone. Rachel was at her boyfriend's house, celebrating his parents' anniversary. She also got engaged that night. On her way home, Rachel misjudged a curve in the road and overcorrected her vehicle, causing it to flip. She was wearing the shoulder strap of her seatbelt under her arm, which allowed her body to fly out of the car. She hit her head on the sunroof, breaking her neck. I will never forget where I was when I got the call. For me, one of the most challenging parts of dealing with her death was thinking about her as she lay on the wet, cold ground, dying in pain. There was comfort in knowing without a shadow of a doubt she was home in heaven, and one day, I would see her again. But this did not take away the pain of thinking she suffered alone while trying to take her last breaths.

The Windsor's came to handle all the details that need to be addressed when someone dies. After identifying her body, they wanted to see where the accident happened. When they arrived at the spot, they immediately saw that someone had erected a small cross. Attached to the cross was a letter explaining how a group of people had been hunting early in the morning and came upon Rachel after she crashed. They called for help, and as they waited for the rescue team, they knelt beside my sister, held her hand, and offered her comfort and prayer in her last moments. She did not die alone. God had sent angels to be with her as she left this world and entered her eternal one. When I heard about and saw the letter, I bawled—not from anger, pain, or loss but from relief and comfort.

When Rachel died, everything changed for all of us. Her death felt like the loose thread on the hem of your favorite skirt. As it hangs and rubs against your leg, it irritates your skin. You lean down, and in haste, you pull on that thread. You rip it, but in the midst of trying to alleviate and remove what should not be there, you unravel the hem around the bottom of the skirt. What started as a small thread out of place is now a much bigger mess. You are unsure if it can be fixed or repaired or if you have just ruined your skirt forever. You have hope that you or someone with more knowledge of how to fix a frayed hem will be able to make it look close to new again. But until it's repaired, you are sad and even mad at what may never be again.

After Rachel died, Charles and Diana divorced. The details of who did what to whom and when they did those things are not my story to tell. All that is important here is how this impacted me, my beliefs about marriage, and especially who I thought I was. This was just another time when I felt deserted. Charles made choices that influenced me far beyond what he probably ever knew or understood.

After the divorce, he moved across the country and eventually remarried, and our relationship has never been the same. There were, once again, periods without any communication. Months turned into years, and even though I was now an adult and had a part to play in this on-and-off, up-and-down roller-coaster of a relationship, I saw this distance as rejection. For protection, I closed off my heart and built up a fortress between him and me because I promised myself I would not let him hurt me again. But now we are now rebuilding trust with each other. I am hopeful as we chip away at the protective barriers that divide us from having the father-daughter relationship we both desire.

Diana is remarried to a wonderful man whom we all adore. She has continued to love and support me as one of her own through all the good, bad, ugly, and beautiful in my life. I consider her my spiritual mother and know I can always count on her, even when I don't deserve it. Scarlet now has three children of her own. She is married to a man who had three of his own children, and they are working hard to blend their families. William is married, has three biological children, and has just adopted a fourth child.

Reflection Questions For Section 1

1. Reflect on the Biblical story of Joseph, Genesis 37-50, who experienced betrayal and brokenness at the hands of his own family. How did Joseph's faith sustain him during his darkest moments? How can the concept of God using what was intended for harm for good inspire hope for your own journey of healing?

2. Consider how surrendering to God's fatherly love can fill the void left by an absent parent. How does knowing God as a loving Father help mend brokenness caused by earthly relationships? Do you believe God loves you, unconditionally, more than any person ever could, including your parents? Can you understand what you believe and feel about your earthly father, plays a role in what you believe and how you feel about God? What steps would you need to take in order to believe that a relationship with God is the safest, most loving relationship you will ever have?

3. What coping mechanisms did you develop to navigate feelings of abandonment and rejection? To navigate challenging family situations? How have these coping mechanisms influenced your relational patterns? How might prayer, a relationship with Jesus and

support from a Christian counselor or coach aid in breaking free from your harmful coping mechanisms?

4. Have you experienced any form of trauma or abuse, and if so, how has it impacted your ability to trust and feel safe in relationships? How has this impacted your sense of identity and self-worth? What steps have you taken to heal from the trauma or abuse? Do you believe having a relationship with Jesus Christ can bring healing and restoration? Why or why not?

5. Consider how surrendering to God's love and protection can counteract feelings of shame and guilt resulting from the abuse. What steps can you take to surrender the burden of unforgiveness toward your abuser to God? How does surrendering to God's command to forgive enable you to experience freedom and release from bondage?

SECTION 2

SEARCHING FOR ACCEPTANCE

"Why do you spend silver on what is not food, and your wages on what does not satisfy?"

Isaiah 55:2a (CSB)

CHAPTER 7

God & Church

My introduction to church and God started when we moved to Napa. When I was 8, Mom started taking us to First Christian Church. I went to Sunday school, helped in the nursery, acted in the Christmas plays, and attended various social events. I listened to Bible stories about Cain and Able, Noah's Ark, Jonah and the whale, Daniel and the lions' den, and even the miracles of Jesus. I was baptized in May of 1979 alongside my mother and sister. I understood Jesus is God who became man and never sinned. He was tortured and hung on the cross, and he rose three days later and then went to heaven. However, I never read my Bible outside of church; it didn't feel real to me, and at the time, it was difficult to understand. I am unsure if we prayed at home; maybe we did at the dinner table but never in public. No one ever taught or explained to me what it looked like to have a personal relationship with God the Father, Jesus our Lord, or the Holy Spirit.

My most treasured experiences from these years were attending church camp every summer at Mt. Gilead in Sonoma County. I started going in fourth grade and continued until sixth grade. We had so much fun. The camp was split with the boys' cabins on one side of the creek and the girls' cabins on the other side. Each cabin was like a little magical house made of wood with bunk beds lining each side. They had cutouts for windows and yellow plastic curtains hung to protect us from the sun. On the first day of camp, the leaders formed teams. Each team consisted of a girls' cabin and a boys' cabin. We competed in events all week and received points for first, second, and third place. We competed in typical racing games, Bible verse speed hunting, talent shows, and the cleanest decorated cabin. You were allowed to use masking tape and make designs on the doors and yellow plastic curtains. I remember we made sure our sleeping bags were made each day, pillows tucked inside, nap sacks tucked under the bunks, and floors swept. We also used rocks and stones to create gardens and walking paths to our cabin entrance. At the end of the week, the winning team won an ice cream party with a banana split the size of a football field.

The stars always looked much brighter, shinier, and closer at camp. All the campers and counselors would gather around the amphitheater fire each night to sing songs and talk about God. Forty plus years later I can still recall those special songs: "Peace Like a River," "Oh You Can't Get to Heaven," "Awesome God," "He's Got the Whole World in His Hands," and "My Rock My Sword My Shield." There was also fun in the mess hall. The best part was anticipating a letter from home. You always felt so special and loved when you received a letter from your parents or family. My mom, Grandma Lucy, and Aunt Anna would send me letters. When you heard your name called, you would stand up, hold your head high, and walk as proudly as possible to grab those from the camp counselor. When you returned to your table, you would tear open your letter, not just hoping to read "How it is going?" and "We miss you" and "Have fun" but also looking for a few dollars you could trade at the snack shack for candy. Warning though: you did not want too many letters on the same day, or you had to sing in front of everyone. Other highlights of camp included canoeing in the Russian River, swimming at the beach in Jenner, horseback riding, swimming in the pool, hiking the woods, and meeting friends from all over California.

My favorite part of camp was having my best friend, Korie, with me. We always managed to be in the same cabin every year. The camp was also where I had my first crush. I was taller than him, but then again, I was three inches taller than everyone in fourth, fifth, and sixth grade. We snuck out and met in the middle of the night and shared a kiss or two. Looking back, I got so scared hearing all the weird sounds in the woods at night. We each had our tiny little flashlights trying to direct our steps. I was afraid of bears and lions or getting caught and in trouble with the counselors, but I was most fearful of getting poison oak again. It is hard to avoid leaves of three when you are unsure where you are walking.

A few things happened at our church that put a bad taste in my mouth. My mom wanted to start a Christian singles group, but the pastors told her this wasn't in line with their image or vision for the church. Another incident involved a lady who had played piano for the church for years, but one day, without warning, her husband left her. The church leaders told her that because she was now a divorcee, she could no longer be a part of the worship team and play on Sundays. Friends acted one way on Sundays at church and another way during the week at school. After sixth grade, I was unsure what church was supposed to be or how God fit into my life. I believed being a Christian meant you were a hypocrite.

As I got older, I thought God was someone who judged me, scolded me, and then punished me for my bad behavior. I could picture Him sitting high on His throne, above the world among the clouds, with a gavel in one hand, ready to come down at any of my wrong words or actions. I went to Him only when I needed Him to fix my mistakes or save me from the consequences of my actions. I begged Him to make my life better, help me in some way, and take away the deep pain and loneliness I often felt. I also asked Him why I was so unlovable. If and when I believed He cleaned up my messes or answered my questions to my liking, I went on about my way, doing life according to Heidi, not according to His Word and His truth.

CHAPTER 8

Grammar School & JR High

I always believed I had to perform and be the best to earn the love I craved, wanted, and needed. If I did not think I could be the best or wasn't the best at something, I stopped, quit, or gave up. I was so scared to fail. When I started something new, I would begin with so much hope and determination. I would resolve that this time, this thing would be what I would follow through with, excel at, accomplish, and be a star in. The problem was no matter how hard I tried, I still felt the same. It was like I was never satisfied. I was constantly disappointing myself and letting myself down. I was chasing after the things of this world where I thought I would find something or someone to make me feel worthy of love.

When I was in third grade, my mom decided I needed an outlet for my energy. She told me I was always trying to be the center of attention. Duh! I wanted to be noticed, loved, and accepted by those around me who were supposed to love me without fail. She signed me up for a local Children's Theatre group. We would meet regularly to learn theater techniques and practice for a large production. There were singers, dancers, and then the general actor population. Some people were able to act, sing, and dance. These people are what the theater industry calls a "triple threat." That was not me ... well, not at first. You were usually classified in order from strongest talent to weakest. My order was actor, dancer, and then singer—and by a singer, I do not mean soloist but "stick her in the choir with other kids" singer.

Once the play for the season was chosen, you would audition for the part you wanted. Once cast in a part, you would practice and learn your lines, steps, and blocking (a theatre term for where and when you belong on the stage). After weeks and weeks of practice and preparation, the show was ready for opening day.

My first play with the theater group was *Peter and the Wolf*. I was cast as one of the ducks. My costume was a bright yellow body suit, and on my back were "feathers" made of multi-colored rows of tulle. I wore orange slipcovers for my webbed feet and an orange face mask shaped like a duckbill

When it was time for our part, the music started, and we waddled out on stage doing the practiced steps. Mid-way through our part, the music stopped, even though we were not done with our routine. I was the lead duck, and after pausing a moment, I looked at the other ducks behind me, and said, "Follow me." I continued as if there was still music. Once we finished, I led the other ducks off stage. The audience erupted with applause and whistles. I was smiling from ear to ear as I heard the noises rise and ring throughout the theatre. Right then, I was hooked. I felt seen, noticed, and rewarded for my performance.

After the show, we met backstage to review the night's performance. The director asked the lead duck to stand up. That was me! Before the entire cast, crew, and parents, the director said I did the right thing by staying in character. He praised me for doing my part to ensure the show went on. I was told what I did mattered, was necessary, and "saved" the show.

At Children's Theatre, I was introduced to dancing. The choreographer was a small-framed woman with dark hair always pulled back in a bun. She was exactly as you would picture a Russian ballet teacher to be. (I don't know if she was actually from Russia, but that is how I imagine her now.) She was soft yet stern, and she allowed me to blossom in many dancing roles in the plays. I felt graceful. If you knew me as a child, you would know I was the opposite of smooth and silky. I was tall and thin and often tripped over my own feet. But something happened to me when I was dancing. It was as if

I became someone else. That is why acting and dancing were so appealing to me. I could transform into someone other than myself—maybe someone whom I thought I wanted to be. I could escape the person I believed was unlovable, unworthy, and unwanted. And because I was good at it, I got the attention and acknowledgment that I so desperately desired.

I continued to be part of the Children's Theatre through my senior year of high school. Over the years, I participated in many plays, including *The Music Man*, *Peter Pan*, *Pinocchio*, *Oliver Twist*, *The Wizard of Oz*, and *The Sound of Music*. For the last production, I was Frenchie in *Grease*. I loved it and cannot remember a time when I did not want to be involved.

Another area I searched to be seen and accepted in was modeling. Modeling is not the career to go into if you have low self-esteem or thin skin. According to my mom, ever since I was little, people would approach her and say how beautiful I was. They would point out features like my big brown eyes or my long legs as I got older. My first introduction to modeling was with a small modeling studio in Napa. I received coaching on how to pose in front of the camera, walk on the runway, and present myself in a model-like fashion. After that, I took classes in San Francisco with an agency. The premise is you pay for classes, and as you are learning, they will book you on go-sees and auditions. For the price of classes, you get to take photos and make a portfolio. As time passed, I discovered my look was more commercial than high fashion. That was okay with me because I liked acting anyway. I had several auditions over the years, but nothing panned out. I never got booked. Usually, there is no explanation, though sometimes, right to your face, they would tell you that your nose was too big, your hair was too curly, and your eyes were too far apart. For some models, this was the fuel that made them fight harder. But not me. It was another area where I felt less than, not adequate or even ugly. So instead of trying harder, I stopped. I did not understand what they were saying about me at the time had nothing to do with me and everything to do with being the right fit for their product. Slowly, I stopped booking calls and going to open auditions. I did nothing to further my career. Why try? No one would ever want me in their commercials or print ads.

Since I believed the real me was never good enough, I never felt like my body was either. I didn't like what I saw when I looked in the mirror. As a child, I was taller than most. I was long, lean, and looked like what some boys called me: an ironing board. I always felt underdeveloped compared to all the other girls. My clothes never fit right. If I bought clothes that fit around the waist, they were too short (high waters). Or if I bought the right length, then the waist was too big and looked sloppy. Other girls called me anorexic or told me I looked like a boy. The worst comment was in high school when a girl used to call me "Bee Sting." She usually did this in front of the popular boys.

From an early age, I thought the attention of boys and men was where I got my self-worth and acceptance. I felt awkward when I was alone at parties or dance clubs or just hanging out with friends. I hated the empty feeling of being invisible. I wanted to be noticed, desired, and sought after everywhere I went. If boys flirted with me, courted me, dated me, slept with me, or showed any sign of being attracted to me, then I felt wanted, needed, loved, and whole. It led me to do and say things I became ashamed of, things I would never have dreamed of doing.

I was in fourth grade when I first wanted to be noticed by boys. I stopped thinking of them as my buddies and started wanting them to like me in a way I thought mattered. Using my body was one way I decided to get their attention. My first real kiss happened while playing hide and seek with a neighbor boy. After the kiss, there was no conversation about it, and it never happened again. I had a few crushes on boys in grammar school, but I was convinced I was not the girl anyone wanted to date. My suspicions were confirmed at the sixth-grade roller skating party. A boy I had a crush on asked me out, not just for a slow dance but to be his girlfriend. I was so excited. But by the end of the skating party, he revealed he didn't want to be my boyfriend; instead, some of his friends paid him five dollars to ask me out. OUCH! Crushed, I skated as fast as I could to the bathroom and cried. Even though I was a mess inside, I made sure no one saw me break down, and I pretended like it was no big deal.

My next experience with boys was in junior high. We all know and remember what a torturous time this can be. Ages 12 through 14 are some rough emotional years, especially for those of us who depend on our peers to tell us what we are worth. When no boys liked me or asked me to go steady or dance or kiss behind the backstop, I was sure everything was wrong with me. I was trying to figure out why no one wanted to do these things with me. I assumed it was because of my lack of body development, my short hair, my taller-than-all-the-boys height, my not being a better athlete, and my crooked front teeth. I thought these things, all of which I had no control over, were flaws and shortcomings, and I felt overwhelming shame and rejection.

Chapter 9

High School

M y first sexual experience happened when I was a freshman in high
school. The boy was a senior. He was athletic and played sports,
and even though he was not part of the in-crowd, he was still known
around campus. The night I lost my virginity, we took a drive in his
pickup to a place not far from town known as the spot for making out.
He pulled off the main road, parked, and we hopped out of the truck and
into the bed. I anticipated we would be making out at some point, but
I was surprised by the totality of what would happen. He had brought a
sleeping bag with him. At the time, I told myself that was nice. I mean,
who wants to lie down, look at the stars, and make out on a hard, dirty
truck bed?

As we made out, things started to progress quickly. He moved his hands
all over my body and before I knew it, he removed my pants and panties. No
words were ever spoken. There were no questions asked, like "Do you want
to go all the way?", "Are you ready?" or "Have you ever done this before?" He
just thrusted himself inside of me. There was no part of this that I was ready
for, nor I can look back and say my first time was enjoyable. It felt like it was
happening in slow motion and yet so fast at the same time. Before I knew it,
he finished, rolled off me, and started getting dressed. So I did the same. There
was still no conversation and no concern for me or my feelings physically,

mentally, or emotionally. After our clothes were on again, we packed up and headed back to town.

He suggested we head to the local country club and sneak in for a night swim. We had to stop at my house and grab my swimsuit and a towel. I gathered my things and headed into the bathroom to change. That is when I saw the mess in my pants. There was blood everywhere. I was not sure how I was going to go swimming while I was bleeding, but I just pretended nothing was happening, and I proceeded to get back in the truck. When we arrived at the pool, we walked in as if we belonged there and started swimming. The time at the pool felt awkward. I was nervous about him touching me anymore that night or discovering I was bleeding. After the illegal plunge in the pool, he took me home, gave me a kiss in the front seat of his truck, I opened the door and went inside my house.

I didn't tell anyone about that night, not even my mom. I walked around dazed and confused for a few days as I tried to process what really happened. I had questions I needed answers to, but I felt I had no one to tell or share my experience with. None of what I was going through looked like or reminded me of all the love stories I saw in movies or read about in all my books. I felt so alone when I thought I should have felt the most loved. It didn't help that his only concern after that night was the condition of his sleeping bag—not me, my feelings, or our relationship. At the time I believed once he got what he wanted he had no more use for me. I told myself that I was not good enough, worthy, or really lovable and that my body was all I had to give.

Between my freshman and junior years, I didn't have a steady boyfriend, though not because I didn't try. At the core of everything I did—every sport I played, every class I took, every activity I participated in on and off campus, and every party I attended—I was only there to find the one or have the one find me. Desperate to be like all the other girls, or what I thought all the other girls were, I would say and do things I didn't really want to say or do. The problem was none of these things ever worked, or gave me what I thought they would: acceptance, identity, and love.

The May before my junior year I met a boy, Matthew, while shopping at Macy's department store. He was 18, and I was 16. Matthew was preparing for college, and he planned to play baseball for whatever school he ended up choosing. He drove a small white Toyota pickup with a bat hanging in the rear window. I remember all the times we shared as amazing, especially our first trip to the beach together. When we got there, we walked in the late afternoon drizzle along the wet sand, holding hands and kissing. After the walk, we stood next to his truck listening to music, me facing him, his arms around my waist. In the background, I heard Madonna's song "Crazy for You." I stepped back and sang along. I was using the lyrics to tell him I was in love with him.

The first time we were intimate was at his parents' house. Matthew laid a mattress out on the floor in the front room and had candles lit. To me, this was special—nothing like my first time! He went slow, asked me questions, and ensured I was comfortable and enjoying myself. I was surprised at how nice it felt. Even though this was special and felt good, I had no clue what I was doing or what was supposed to happen. Sharing myself with him this way made me believe we would be together forever. I thought this was the beginning of us, and our happily ever after would follow, just like in my books and movies.

As summer approached, Matthew began finalizing his plans to attend school. I dreaded this and spent every moment I could with him. This did not make his parents happy at all. They approached him with an ultimatum to break it off with me and concentrate on his responsibilities or lose the financial help he needed from them to pay for college. He wanted to play ball and go away more than anything. He loved me, but he knew he could not lose his parents' financial support. So he broke up with me before he left in August. I cried and cried and was so devastated. All our plans—my plans—were ripped from us. Here I was again, alone, rejected, and believing I wasn't worthy. I was convinced if I was prettier, skinnier, more intelligent, more affluent, more fill-in-the-blank, he would have chosen me.

My junior year was my hardest, most challenging, most rebellious year of high school. After the breakup with Matthew, I did not care about playing sports, getting good grades, or trying to move forward. I was in self-destructive mode, hunting for my next love and doing whatever it took to find him.

I started hanging out with a new girl. She was a year older than me, was from out of town, and was a little "naughty." She got me to do and experience things I knew I should not be involved in. She had a boyfriend at the rival high school in town, and he had a cousin, so the four of us started hanging out together. I compromised more and more of myself and my values to feel wanted, accepted, and loved.

When I didn't give this guy everything he wanted, he dumped me. As always, I blamed myself for not being good enough, pretty enough, or loose enough to get or keep a guy. In my mind, it was always my fault, and I would have to adjust my values and beliefs to do whatever it took next time to attract and keep a guy interested in me, loving me, wanting me. This was the pattern of my junior year: boy after boy, one after another, compromise after compromise, looking for someone who could plug the holes in my heart and soul.

I had a great senior year, but I was still tortured by the need to be with someone, to have a boyfriend. I had crushes and guys whom I went on dates with, but nothing since my first love was ever the same. In January 1988, I was on track to go away to College of the Siskiyous in Weed, California in the fall. My grades were back up, and I was playing sports again, hanging with my favorite people, and doing all the senior activities. Being popular and feeling like I was the center of attention made me feel special and accepted, so I got lots of pleasure and fulfillment from being involved.

Some highlights and very fond memories of that year were playing volleyball as front row blocker and winning third runner up, physical fitness, and Miss Congeniality at the Junior Miss Scholarship contest. I was awarded scholarships for academics and other achievements and nominated by SADD as their homecoming candidate. I served on the student council, made good grades, and went to concerts (the best was the Def Leppard concert in San Francisco with one of my besties I had known since fourth grade-Marie).

Just before Christmas, the boy I had dated my freshman year—the one whom I lost my virginity to—came knocking. He was on leave from the Navy. When I answered the door, there he stood, looking more muscular and handsome than my freshman year. He looked like a grown man, like the hunks from the movie *Top Gun*. I was overtaken with mixed emotions and feelings. I wanted to jump in his arms and run away happily ever after, but simultaneously, I was upset, scared, and confused about why he was even here. I do not remember the conversation or the details of how we ended up on a date, but we were sitting at the movie theatre watching Eddie Murphy's *RAW*. As the movie played, we kissed and touched. I remember thinking, *Wow, an older boy wants to be with me! He came back to me because he wants to make everything right that went wrong the first time.* Here was my second chance to have the relationship I wanted the first go around

After the movie, he drove me over to his father's apartment. We ended up making out on the floor, and at some point, he started to undo my pants. I told him I did not want to have sex, but he did not listen or stop. He used the weight of his body to hold my hands down above my head as he proceeded to do what he wanted to do. I did not scream, yell, or put up a fight. I just lay there, convincing myself this must be normal. I checked out emotionally and mentally as I looked past his face. Once he was finished, he let go of my hands, rolled off me, stood up, and got dressed. I stood up, pulled up my pants, and used the bathroom to clean up. There was no talk or conversation about what had taken place. I have no memory of how I got home or how the night ended.

For weeks I was confused, angry, sad, and depressed. I was very tired and had no energy. After not getting my period, I believed the worst thing had happened: I believed I had gotten pregnant. Ashamed, embarrassed, and feeling so alone, all I kept saying to myself was, *How on earth am I going to be able to go away to college? How can I walk at graduation pregnant?* I worried that no boy would ever love me or marry me if I had a baby. All I could think about was how this pregnancy was nothing I wanted and nothing I deserved.

During this time I missed school, didn't leave the house, and didn't shower or even get dressed some days. My mom guessed the reason for the drastic change in my behavior and took me to Planned Parenthood. We walked in, and everyone was excited my mom had come with me for support. I took a urine test and was escorted into a back room, where they gave me the news that I was indeed pregnant. They asked if I understood what that meant and what I wanted to do about it. I shared my concerns, worries, and fears about being pregnant at 17, and the next thing I knew, I had an appointment scheduled for an abortion. There was never a discussion about the different options available to me, not from the woman at Planned Parenthood or even my mom. She kept telling me she would support whatever decision I made. We never prayed about it, talked to a pastor, looked at adoption, or talked about what it might look like to raise a baby starting at 17. I got no help from anyone. I had to make this very adult, grown-up decision on my own.

The day came to get the "procedure" done. That morning, we drove to the facility which was over an hour away. When we got out of the car and walked toward the front door, we had to pass men and women holding signs telling me that I was killing my baby, that I was a murderer. I couldn't get past them fast enough. Once inside, I had to fill out paperwork and wait for the staff to call me back. When it was my turn, they took me alone, asked me if I knew why I was there, explained the procedure in detail, and asked for my consent to move forward. How can a child consent to this critical decision? How did they believe that at 17, I was able to comprehend the full extent of my decision? Why did they think I would understand the lasting consequences of this action?

Someone walked me to a different room where I changed out of my clothes and laid down on an exam table. I can recall there being two nurses and a doctor who performed the abortion. Within minutes, it was over. I was given instructions for aftercare, and then I got dressed. They escorted me to the room where my mom was waiting to take me home. Mom could not sit silently; she wanted to know all the details. The problem was I didn't want to talk. But as always, I was more worried about how she was feeling about what just happened, so I pretended to be strong and recounted the events to her.

The next day, I thought I was dying because I was bleeding out clots the size of half dollars. My mom did not know what to think or how to help, so she drove me to the ER, where I had to explain to the receptionist, nurses, and doctors that just two days prior I had an abortion. I continued to act as if it was no big deal, answering questions easily like water rolling off a duck's back. But on the inside, I was mortified that anyone other than my mom was going to know. After a few days, my life returned to normal. The abortion was swept under the rug, in good company with the other family secrets.

Before becoming pregnant and having an abortion, I had gone on a campus tour of College of the Siskiyous with Korie. While there, I ran into my ex-boyfriend Matthew, the love of my life from the summer before my junior year. I had no idea he had chosen the same campus as me, but there he was. It was as if lightning had come down from heaven and struck me right where I stood. I was sure I was seeing a ghost and not the person I had dreamed of being together forever with. I was dazed and confused, trying to sort out my feelings. I was weak in the knees, waiting for him to give me some signal, hoping he missed me as much as I missed him. He hugged me and told me he had missed me so much. Over the next few days, we hung out, talked, and even kissed. Before leaving for home, we decided to be boyfriend and girlfriend again, despite his parents' wishes for him to stay single to concentrate on his education.

Over the next four months, we had a long-distance relationship. During this time, I learned I was pregnant and had the abortion. Matthew would visit me when he could, write letters, call, make me mixed tapes of love songs, and send me small gifts in the mail. At one point, he even bought me a small ring to symbolize his seriousness about our future together. But by early May, he could not handle the pressure from his parents about us dating, and once again, he broke up with me. This time, it was more than challenging. It was a gut punch that left me feeling like there was no hope. After all, I thought finding the right guy who wanted to be with me forever meant I would finally be whole and loved, wanted and desired. I felt like I gave up so much for him, including my baby. I was sure I was destined to be alone forever.

CHAPTER 10

College Beginnings

Summer seemed to fly by, and I packed up for college in the fall. At the last minute, Korie decided not to go away with me to the same school. I felt blindsided, confused, hurt, and scared to be on this new adventure without her. Even though part of me didn't want to go alone, I went anyway.

During the first few days on campus, I attended freshman orientation. I learned about the campus rules: where I was allowed to go and not go, when to eat, what classes to take, who could come in the dorms, when my curfew was, and all the pertinent details to keep me out of the dorm mother's room and out of trouble. These were not the only things I learned. This is the first time and place I had heard about date rape. They explained what it was, how it happens, how often it occurs, and what to do if you think this happens to you on campus. I sat there stunned at what I was hearing. According to what they were telling me, this is precisely what had happened to me when I lost my virginity and the night I became pregnant—both times with the same boy. I was not sure what I was supposed to do with this newfound information. It brought up a flood of feelings I was not sure how to handle. Was I supposed to tell someone? What about a friend, my mom, the dorm rep, or a school nurse or counselor? I convinced myself that my experience was probably not date rape (or maybe, worst case, nonconsensual) and that it had not—would not!— affect the rest of my life.

I was lying to myself again about what I could and couldn't handle, forever playing the strong child so as not to upset or be a burden to anyone, especially my family or Mom. I knew that if I had told her this, she would freak out, blame herself, and make it about her. I went along about my business of juggling classes, dancing, acting, trying to fit in and find friends, and finding a boy to call my own. After all, who was I unless I had a significant other? I believed the answer was *nobody*. This insecurity led me to continue to allow myself to do things I knew I should not be doing. Wasn't one pregnancy and abortion enough to scare me into keeping my panties on? Nope.

After my first semester away, I decided not to return in the spring. Instead, I attended a semester at Napa Junior College and then transferred to a different school thirty minutes away. A year after that, I moved even farther away with a few friends from high school. I waited tables as I concentrated on finishing up and, of course, finding my other half. Still interested in medicine, I switched it up to pursue a nursing degree. I told myself I was not willing to put off marriage until after med school. I was sure being a doctor meant I would not be able to get married or have children until after I was in my mid-thirties. Back then, I thought that was too old.

I got a job as a waitress at a fancy Italian restaurant in "Old Town." I was working, making good money, and doing life as a young college student. I was still up to my shenanigans trying to find someone to love me the way I thought I needed to be loved. I was looking at work, at school and hunting at bars that I could sneak into, at the gym, and at my apartment complex. My goals were not about me and my future unless it involved getting a boyfriend. As you can imagine, this means I made some bad choices with the men I was meeting. I continued to believe that to get a man to like me, I had to give myself to him physically, no matter how early on in the relationship, no matter the consequences or the risks. In these first few years, there were dates and guys I had crushes on, men I had casual affairs with, and lots of disappointment and shame. I continued to believe I was not good enough, not lovable, and not wanted. I was convinced that I was damaged goods. The more shame and disgust I had for myself, the more I thought the only way to feel better was to get someone to love me. It was a never-ending pit of shame and regret.

CHAPTER 11

Before I Said "I Do"

I was attending Santa Rosa Junior College, taking classes towards my Associate in Science degree, and getting ready to enter their nursing program. One of the prerequisites for this program was having work experience in a hospital or nursing home, or you could have an EMT certificate. I did not want to work in a nursing home, and I didn't have enough experience to get hired at the hospital. I thought it would be cool to get my EMT certificate. At the beginning of the semester, we formed study groups to help absorb all the information and ensure we could pass both the written and practical tests. I joined a group that included a guy named Mark. After a few study sessions, it suddenly hit me: I was interested in this guy! Mark seemed nice, we were in the same class, and I thought he was cute. I decided to take a chance and invite him out for a date to the Tightwad Tuesday movies, and he accepted.

Mark was shocked when he came to my door to pick me up for our date. I usually attended class in the evenings with my hair in a ponytail or a bun, having come straight from working or working out. He had only ever seen me very casually dressed, but for this date, I put on nice clothes and makeup and wore my hair down with my natural curls. After the movie, *Little Man Tate*, we drove to his parents' house. As we approached, I asked him, "Oh, which apartment is yours?" Mark laughed at me and said, "It's all ours." His parents' house was a very long ranch-style home with so many windows that

I thought it was an apartment building. Nope! It was just a house with five bedrooms, three bathrooms, an office, a formal dining room, a formal living room, and a den. We headed to his room was above the garage. It was a typical guy's room with posters on the wall and clothes on the floor. Of course, we lay down on the bed and started talking, which led to making out. This was the start of our fifteen-year relationship.

After a few dates, we became sexual. After six short months of dating, we moved in together. I was sure this meant we would be planning our dream wedding, getting married, starting our careers, beginning a family, and living happily ever after. We never talked about the hopes, dreams, desires, or expectations we had about our relationship, each other, or our future. We just moved in and started playing house, ignoring or not knowing the important conversations we should have had.

Since I was never raised in a home with a man or brothers, there were many surprises after moving in with a man for the first time. I had no idea men left the toilet seat up and that if you walked into the bathroom at night and did not turn on a light or double check the seat, you would plunge into the bowl. There were sounds and smells that came from Mark's body that I was sure were the soundtrack for scary movies. The things he did were foreign, troubling, and even shocking. I had no idea how to handle them or how to talk to him about how I felt.

I always took Mark's emotional temperature to ensure he was okay and had what he needed and wanted. I cleaned the house the way he wanted, cooked foods he liked, went to restaurants he preferred, and hung out with the friends he chose. He never asked me to give up anything of mine; I just did that on my own, thinking that was how it was supposed to be. For him to love me, I had to be who I thought he wanted me to be. The real me was not good enough.

I also had assumptions about how Mark wanted me to look, act, smell, dress, and talk—none of which was the real me. I became a fake version of myself, never speaking up because I didn't want to upset him or make waves. I was always afraid that at any moment he would discover the real me and run the other direction. Sure, there were glimpses of me that would push through the cracks of my façade, but most of the time, I was putting on a show. This led me to make things up, stretch the truth, and lie. I lied about who I was, what I did, things I saw, and anything I felt would make him love me more. I never gave him the chance to like me for me.

My real history and the things that happened to me were buried deep. I was afraid to show or tell anyone, let alone the man I wanted to marry, these things. What if I scared him away or made him think less of me? I never shared my fears with him. I never shared the truth about being molested by my cousin or losing my virginity or how many men I had slept with. I never shared how deep the wounds went that my father caused. I skirted around how dysfunctional my family was. I was protective over my secrets and shame, and I kept them all buried deep, partially because I wasn't honest with myself about how these events shaped me.

Mark had no idea how some of his words and actions or inactions affected me. He did not understand my severe reactions to his choices. This was especially true when I would "catch" him looking at porn. He told me it is normal for all boys and men to use porn. He said because I grew up without brothers or a father, I would not understand this was normal behavior. But it did not feel normal to me. It felt perverted and disgusting, and it triggered thoughts about what happened all those years ago with my cousin.

Of course, I internalized all of this. After all, if this was "normal" behavior, then these were normal girls and women, and the sex he was watching was normal. I compared myself to those girls in those movies, and guess what? I did not look or act like any of them. So yet again I believed I was not good enough and could never measure up to what I thought he wanted. If he was into those magazines and girls, I told myself that must be what he wanted. Every time I found porn hidden under our mattress or a video tucked away in a closet, I started to spiral. I tried to keep all the disgusting feelings pushed down, submerged as far as I could, but when I least expected it, they would break free. Then I would cry and protest and tell Mark how it made me feel, and he would promise to stop. He would buy me flowers and tell me all the things I wanted to hear. The problem was this pattern repeated itself for most of our relationship, and when someone tells you one thing but does another, you tend not to believe them.

Mark and I both brought a ton of baggage into our relationship, and no one showed us how to unpack it in a healthy way. Over the years we tried to do it on our own, but we struggled to communicate, like so many couples do. I took everything he said personally, internalized it, and added it to the list of reasons I was unlovable and why he would leave at any moment. He avoided confrontation altogether. When he was upset or I was not meeting his needs, he would work on his car, hang out with friends, or escape into porn. Don't get me wrong, though: we had lots of fun together and made many great memories. We both believed we had an okay, good-but-not-perfect relationship.

Reflection Questions For Section 2

1. How do you define acceptance and why is it important to you?

2. Have you ever compromised your values or beliefs in search of acceptance from others?

3. Reflect on a time when you sought acceptance from others rather than fully surrendering to God's acceptance. How did surrendering to God's acceptance change your perspective?

4. Consider the story of the woman at the well (John 4:1-42), who found acceptance and redemption in Jesus despite her past. How does her story resonate with your own search for acceptance?

5. What are some consequences you have had to face or are facing now because of immoral choices you have made? When you look in the mirror do you define yourself by the mistakes and choice you have made? Do you believe God can and will forgive you? Read 1 John 1:9 "If we confess our sins, he is faithful and righteous to forgive us our sins and to cleanse us from all unrighteousness." What does ALL mean to you in this scripture?

6. Would a mentorship or guidance from an older, wiser individual in your church, have helped you make healthier, Godlier choices in your past? If not, what support systems or resources did you rely on during challenging times?

7. How does the story of the prodigal son in Luke 15:11-32 demonstrate God's unwavering love and forgiveness, even in the face of our own mistakes and bad choices?

SECTION 3

MOTHERHOOD & THEN MARRAIGE

"What is the source of wars and fights among you? Don't they come from your passions that wage war within you? You desire and you do not have. You murder and covet and cannot obtain. You fight and wage war. You do not have because you do not ask. You ask and don't receive because you ask with wrong motives, so that you may spend it on your pleasures."

James 4:1-3(CSB)

CHAPTER 12

A Baby Will Change Everything

By the time I was 23, I had an itch to start a family. I was sure this was the natural progression of any relationship: get married, have babies, and live happily ever after. Mark had just finished the firefighter academy at the beginning of 1994. I was sure he would have asked me to marry him by now. When that did not happen, I thought everything would change if we had a baby. That would seal the deal, and the moment he found out, he would drop to one knee and ask me for my hand in marriage. I would have it all, and life would be just how I always dreamed it could be.

Well, it didn't take long after I stopped using birth control to become pregnant. I was so happy but at the same time terrified. I knew I had to muster up the courage to tell Mark. When I sat down and told him, his response was not what I expected or wanted. His words are etched in my brain forever: "Well, next time, we will have to be more careful."

I asked him what that meant, even though I knew deep in my soul what he was saying. He meant I should have an abortion, explaining, "We always said now is not a good time to get pregnant."

I answered back, "But I never said if we did get pregnant that I would abort the baby."

I was mortified that Mark would ever suggest such a thing, and I was angry at myself for thinking this plan of mine would work. One thing I knew for sure was I was not going to kill another baby growing inside of me, no matter what. After the dust settled and Mark had time to accept the fact we were having a baby, we started telling our parents and closest friends that we were pregnant. The baby was due at the end of October. No one seemed surprised or concerned. Maybe they all assumed, as I did, that we were on our way to being married anyway, so no biggie.

Our first child was going to be born with a job: to make his dad want to stay with me, marry me, and love me. That was not the only job I gave the baby, though. It also had the big responsibility to be someone who would love me unconditionally, no matter what. This baby wasn't even born yet, and the weight I was placing on those little shoulders was immense. I was desperate to fill the holes in my heart and soul.

During the pregnancy, Mark's parents gifted us a diamond ring, and he gave it to me. We were in his mother's closet, where she kept her jewelry. She handed me the ring, and it went on my finger. There was no romantic proposal, but finally we were engaged, and we started planning a wedding. I only cared about *not* being a big, pregnant bride walking down the aisle. I still wanted to have a dream wedding with all the traditional stuff, and I was not about to settle for going down to City Hall—baby in belly—saying, "I do," and calling it good. We all thought we should wait until after the baby was born.

I was over the moon when my firstborn was a boy. We named him Luke. Since I was little, I have always wanted to be a boy's mom. In the early 1990s, it was still not unheard of to go into labor and not know the sex of your baby. I wanted it to be a surprise. Some of my joy that our baby was a boy was also for Mark. I believed if I could give him a son, it would cement our relationship. If it was a girl, I was scared that Mark would take one look, blame me for having a girl baby and then leave. Sound familiar? Remember, my dad blamed my mom for me being a girl, and I believed that was one of the reasons why my dad left us.

The first eight weeks as a new mother were some of the most brutal weeks of my life. How was this chunky little boy supposed to get Mark to marry me when all he did was eat, sleep, cry, and poop? And to make matters worse, I had a postpartum body that was shocking for me to look at in the mirror, let alone show to Mark. I hated my body and was 100 percent sure I would never be the same again.

When I went to my six-week postpartum checkup, the doctor discovered I had a section of skin that healed with extra skin cells, and they had to use a sulfur stick to burn it off. Let's just say I would rather have given birth again! When I got home, Mark asked me how things went and if the doctor released me to start having sex again. I had to tell him it would be another six weeks. I was sure he was okay with that, though, because I just had another medical procedure. He never seemed to push to have sex or mention any frustrations with having to wait. We never discussed creative ways to alleviate sexual tension and buildup.

It wasn't long until I found pornography hidden somewhere in the house. As always, I stuffed my feelings, internalized them, and blamed myself. But after who knows how long, I blew up at Mark for leaving a dirty dish in the sink, a wet towel on the floor, or the cap off the toothpaste. Obviously, it wasn't really about those things. It was because of what I believed about myself and what I thought Mark was doing to me by using porn. On this occasion, through large reservoirs of tears, I asked why he was looking at porn. His response was typical: "All guys do it, especially after their significant others have a baby." He told me it was better than him going out and cheating on me because he had needs that I was unable to meet. His words made me believe it was entirely my fault he was using porn. I was so confused. I was not able to have sex after the treatment of my lady parts. How was this my fault? Oh yes, I was the one who got pregnant and decided to keep the baby. If I had never had our son, this would not have happened.

At some point, this cycle of dysfunction would complete, and either Mark would apologize and promise never to do it again or we would pretend like it never happened and sweep it under the rug. Well, our emotional rugs started to have piles under them with many hurts, feelings, and issues in those first few years. Why did I allow this? Because I had no idea how to share my feelings or that I was even allowed to. I was always afraid that if and when I spoke about my feelings, Mark would not listen to me, understand me, or empathize with me. He would just say, "Enough is enough!" and leave. So stuffing and sweeping became how I dealt with the unresolved, scary thoughts and feelings that lived inside.

CHAPTER 13

Damaged From The Start

Not long after our first son was born, we were back to wedding planning. From November 1994 to March 1996, our lives consisted of dress shopping, choosing a place to hold the wedding, asking friends and family to stand alongside us in the ceremony, taste testing the food, cake, and drinks, and picking out flowers and decorations. We did most of the planning ourselves and used our own money for most purchases. Grandma Lucy blessed me and bought my dress, and Mark's parents paid for our honeymoon. Besides that, we got creative, and I shopped the sales to help keep the budget low.

Remember how I never had a typical proposal? I would always tell Mark, "If you do not pop the question to me before the wedding, then I will not marry you." I would say it in a joking manner with a little attitude, but of course, I did not mean it. My goal was to be married, so why would I say this? I would have never followed through with my threat. The wedding rehearsal and dinner were night before the wedding. It just so happened this was also my birthday. We were eating and socializing with family, friends, and people in the wedding party when Mark got down on one knee, presented me with a beautiful bouquet, and asked me to marry him.

After the wedding, we went on our honeymoon. When we returned home, life went back to normal. Our son was now almost 18 months old, and Mark was serious about becoming a full-time firefighter. His goal was to work somewhere other than a volunteer department and for the fire extinguisher company. We decided one of the best ways for him to do this was to get his paramedic certificate, and he was accepted into the local junior college program. It was a lot of hard work and sacrifice to get him through the program, with long hours at school and studying for bookwork and practical's. Mark struggled, but we did what we had to do to get through. After he graduated from the program, he started to work on ambulances and fill in at local fire departments.

It was now the mid to late 1990s, and having a computer with internet in your home became a reality. This was the start of giving you or anyone in your home access to almost anything you wanted to know. In our home, this opened up countless opportunities for pornography use without having to hide magazines or movies.

During these years, Mark would also attend bachelor parties. At these events, there were often strippers. I was also told other things were being done in the bathroom or the bedrooms at these parties. When he came home, I would feel disgusted by what I knew, or at least the parts I had heard about. These types of events made me feel worse about myself. In no way did I look like these girls. Most of them had chests made of silicone, wore a size zero, and had long blonde hair. I believed Mark was dreaming, thinking, and fantasizing about these girls, even when we were intimate. I never felt good enough. I would ask and plead my case about him not attending these parties, but I would get the same old story about how all the guys did this. Often, I was called a prude.

Because we were both broken in our own ways with our own flaws, faults, and dysfunctions, we were not doing life and marriage in a healthy way. I was not following God's plan and Mark was not a believer. Neither of us met each other's needs or served or loved each other the way God intended. This is no excuse for my actions and choices or Mark's actions and choices, but it led me to do things that further damaged myself, my husband, my child, and my marriage. I took what should have been only for my husband and shared it with others. I would talk with other men inappropriately, flirt with them, and allow them to kiss me. Worse yet, I became sexual with men outside of my marriage.

Each time I made these choices, small or large, I would feel awful, sneaky, and disgusting. But even so, there was some temporary relief from the desperate feeling of wanting to be loved and desired. I had to lie, hide, and say and do things I was not proud of. Not all these instances were sexual, but they were not how a married woman should be acting. I would go years without stepping outside our marriage, and then it would start again. We had times in our relationship that were great, times that were okay, times that were tough, and times that were terrible. Like any relationship, we had our ups and downs, ins and outs.

CHAPTER 14

Baby Number Two Born With A Job

I n the middle of our dysfunction, in May of 2001, I completed schooling
at Sonoma State University and graduated with honors. Learning was
another way I distracted myself from feeling and dealing with the issues in our
marriage. I was accepted into the teaching program in my senior year. After
graduation, I continued working toward my teaching credential, fulfilling all
the requirements, including my student teaching. I had one assignment left
to turn in, and in true Heidi fashion, I took an incomplete in the class. After
all my hard work, I was one class short of achieving my teaching credential.
Looking back, I can't find any good reason why I did this. Here I was again,
not finishing something, not following through to completion what I had
started.

In August, Mark and I decided to have another baby. Within one month
of me being off the pill, we became pregnant. In my head, I believed having
this second baby would help put our up-and-down marriage back on track.
This small child would save our marriage. Once again, my baby would be
born with a job.

Mark landed his dream job as a firefighter and we bought our first house.
The house we lived in was 1,300 square feet, with three bedrooms, two

baths, a kitchen, living room, laundry room, garage, small front yard, and a backyard. We lived there for a few years, did some minor remodeling, and made basic improvements. It was a cozy, tiny home perfect for our growing family, or so I thought. But Mark wanted a larger place. He always wanted bigger, better, more. This is where our backgrounds from different sides of the tracks collided. I was used to not having much, and he was used to having everything he wanted. This was not a bad thing; it was just what each of us knew.

So there we were with a new baby, and Mark wanted to take a chance and buy a bigger place. The real estate where we were living was costly. At the time, I would have to go back to work full-time for us to get a bigger house, and I did not want to do that. I loved being a stay-at-home mom for the boys. We were unsure how we would both get what we wanted. One day, Mark came home from work and told me that many firefighters lived outside the city. Some even lived outside the state. They would work a group of days together and then go home for a couple of weeks at a time. He suggested we move out of Sonoma County to somewhere more affordable.

This could work, but how far away were we talking? What about our family and friends? Again, Mark came home from work after talking to some other firefighters, and he told me that some of the guys lived in a region northeast of us that gave them a two-hour or so commute. As of now, it took him about the same amount of time to get to work, not because of distance but because traffic was so awful where we lived. We took a day trip and scouted out what we did and did not like about each of the towns we were considering.

We went home, decided to sell our house, and started hunting for another one in this new area. In the meantime, our second son, James, was born. He was a beautiful, large baby. I was a different person for him than I was for Luke. I was calmer, more determined to be present, and set on a mission to breastfeed. When you are distracted by taking care of a newborn, packing to sell a house, showing the home to potential buyers, entertaining and caring for a second grader, and doing daily life, you forget you are unhappy and unhealthy in your marriage. You ignore all the tension and continue to sweep problems under the rug. I can't speak for Mark, but I can guess these new distractions were as much of a relief for him as they were for me. New adventures also brought hope for change in our relationship. It was not a conscious thought that living somewhere else and starting over together would bring us closer and things would be different, but I could feel there was hope in the air.

CHAPTER 15

New Didn't Mean Better

W e found a buyer for our house, and after looking high and low in the new town, we picked an almost 3,000-square-foot house with four bedrooms, three baths, an upstairs and a downstairs, with an aboveground pool on just over an acre of land. It felt like it was in the country, but it was close to shopping and the freeway so Mark would have quick access on his way to work. Moving two hours away was no joke, especially with an 8-month-old baby. We slowly unpacked as we started creating a life in this new house and area. My husband had his new routine where he would work two or three days in a row, so he could be home for lengthier stretches at a time. If you do not know, a firefighter's schedule is different. They do not work Monday through Friday, with eight-hour shifts and weekends off. Usually, the shifts are twenty-four hours on and then forty-eight hours off. In total, Mark worked nine or ten twenty-hour shifts away from home.

I was in a new house in a new town with no friends. I had a baby, an 8 year old, and a husband who was gone three to four days a week. I felt isolated and very alone. Baby James was a great eater but an awful sleeper. He would not stay in his crib, and he barely napped. I was so sleep-deprived. Luke was having some trouble focusing in school. Because he is so intelligent, he easily got bored in class and would start bothering other students and the teachers, wanting to talk or being the class clown. We had to have him tested for ADD/ADHD. Years later, I laugh because as an adult, James is so calm and even-keeled. But back then, raising a child more brilliant than you with more energy than a nuclear power plant was tough.

I did not know it then, but I had terrible postpartum depression. There were days I did not want to get out of bed. I would do what I had to do to make sure the boys were cared for, but I was not caring for myself. I often didn't shower or change my clothes. I would not make healthy food choices, so it was more challenging this time to lose the baby weight, which made me feel like a blob and further spiral into depression. Somehow, I managed to get to a local doctor. She was shocked I had made it this far without harming myself or the boys. She diagnosed me with postpartum depression but also said I was so sleep-deprived that it was making things ten times worse. Add into the mix my feelings of isolation from being in a new town, and she said I was a hot mess of symptoms. She prescribed me an anti-depressant to help regulate me.

After a few months on the meds, I felt so much better. I was slowly thawing the cold shell of a person I had become. I enjoyed setting up the house, and I started exercising regularly. I would go on walks at local parks, lakes, and even our neighborhood. On one such occasion, I met the couple who lived across the street. They had two girls. One was close to Luke's age, and the other was one or two years older than James. This couple asked about our family, where we were from, our jobs, and all the introduction-type questions. The wife was brave and asked me if I went to church. I told her I was a believer, but my husband was not. I also confessed I had not been to a regular church in years. She invited me to come to their church, which was not far from where we lived. I said, "Sure, I will check it out."

One Sunday, I loaded up the boys and headed to the church. It turned out that the father of one of Luke's classmates was the lead pastor. The boys and I went back almost every Sunday. For the first time in a long time (or ever), I was working on myself the way God designed us to work on ourselves: from His Word, His truth, His people, His community, and His worship songs. This church and His people gave me the gift of respite. It was a safe place for the fog of depression and loneliness to evaporate from my inner being. I made friends, joined a women's Bible study, and attended regularly with the boys on Sundays. I was learning what it meant to have a relationship with God, Jesus, and the Holy Spirit, or I was trying anyway. This did not mean my life miraculously changed when I walked through the church doors, but this was where it started—where God showed me glimpses of what could be, what I should be, and who I should be.

Mark and I were settled in, and the distractions of a new house and having a new baby wore off. Our dysfunction started to push its way out of the cracks in our relationship. I felt like a single mother while Mark was away working for days in a row. He would come home and need time to decompress from his time on duty. I understood that some of the calls he went on were brutal, and his hours were long and tough. But I still needed him. I needed my partner to come home to help wrangle children, help with homework, help with activities, and help with discipline. Instead of jumping in and doing the things I needed help with, Mark would busy himself with working in the yard or on his hot rod. I am not saying what he was doing wasn't necessary; it was just not the help I needed. Did I tell him what I needed from him? Nope! I would stuff my concerns, wants, and needs, and then when the pressure built up too much, I would explode. I started getting angry and resentful of our schedule and having to be the one to do it all. The yelling from both sides began to increase in volume and frequency.

CHAPTER 16

I Wanted Out

When James was 2 1/2, Mark and I decided I should get a part-time job. It was supposed to help get me out of the house, meet people, and alleviate me from feeling as if I had no adult interactions. Plus the money would help pay some of the bills. Mark was making good money, but he had things he wanted. When he wanted something, he would buy it. Often, there was no thought about the financial burden on us, and there was little to no discussion with me about purchases. I was often told that because he made the money, he could spend it how he wanted.

I applied and got hired at a local brewery. Of course the place I needed to work was a restaurant full of food, beer, and other unhappy, miserable people drowning their sorrows in so-called fun. I waited tables and worked behind the bar, pouring craft-made brews. At first, just being out of the house and talking to adults fed my soul. I laughed, joked, and met lots of "friends." I use quotation marks because real friends will not tempt you, coerce you, or encourage you to make choices against your marriage vows, family, husband, and children.

By fall of that year, things went from bad to worse. When it happened, I lied to myself and believed what I was doing was best for me and my boys. I was still not honest or upfront, and I never told my husband I was miserable. I never asked to go to counseling or get help from any of the people at church.

The only people I was listening to were me, my so-called friends, and Satan. I continued to believe his lies about who I was, how I got here, and what I should do to remedy my so-called horrible situation and marriage. I often wanted to pack my bags, grab the boys, and head out alone. But one thing that kept me in the house with Mark was wondering how I would survive on my own. How would I pay the bills? I was only working part-time as a waitress. There would have been no way for me to pay rent, utilities, food, and gas on my salary. And I was *not* going to go live with my mom. I felt trapped in my situation.

I was 100 percent sure there was no way out, and this would be my life forever. By this time, Mark was sleeping in the downstairs main bedroom, and I was in an upstairs guest bedroom. We were living like two ships passing in the night. Each of us had activities we did on our own, with an occasional family outing. The tension in the house was thick. The yelling, arguing, name-calling, and avoiding each other became the norm instead of the exception. On the outside, I acted like everything was okay, but on the inside, I was dying. I hated my life and who I was becoming, and I really believed I had no choice in any of it.

The attention from my new friends and strangers at the brewery gave me the sense of belonging, friendship, and companionship I was craving and not getting from my husband. I gave these people my "good" side. The happy-go-lucky Heidi showed up to work, serve, and have fun. It was all one big fat distraction. Some regulars would come into the bar and talk to me about their lives and troubles and want my opinion. People asked me how I was doing and what was happening in my life. Granted, many of them didn't truly care at all, but to me, these new friends made me feel accepted and loved, and this was where I was getting my identity. I was never my true self with them, and I often exaggerated or lied about who I was or things I had done. After all, I did not want these new friends to learn about the real me and not like me. I had to be who I thought they wanted me to be.

By December, I had made some more inappropriate friendships with men. I loved the flirting and banter back and forth; it made me feel desired and wanted. Once again, I crossed the line and took one relationship past the point of no return. I made many brazen choices, almost like I wanted to be caught. Sneaking out after work until one or two in the morning, I was in party mode, and I did not put my children or my marriage before work, or my new friends.

One day, when I was standing in my living room, trying to convince Luke to do homework or a chore, he shouted at me, "Mom, stop being so psycho!"

What did he say to me? He was 10 years old. Where had he heard that word, and why would he call me that? After I calmed down, we talked, and Luke told me that his dad said I was not emotionally well. Apparently, Mark had said I was "psycho" and instructed the kids to be nice to me because upsetting me made me emotional.

WOW! I was not sure what I was more upset at: the fact my husband had a conversation with our 10-year-old about my emotional state, that Luke called me psycho, or that Mark was not disciplining Luke's lousy behavior. At that moment, I made an inner vow to myself that my boys would not be taught how to treat their wives by their father.

I was determined to get out. Again, I did not go to my husband with this. I allowed Satan to use this situation to divide us further. I convinced myself that I did not deserve this kind of treatment and that now was the time to come up with an exit plan. I had no idea what this looked like or when it would happen—I just knew I wanted out.

CHAPTER 17

Kenny in Shinning Armor

I was getting to know another male friend at my job through conversations on his lunch breaks or when he would come in for dinner. His name was Kenny, and I learned he loved the outdoors, skiing, hiking, and mountain biking. We talked a little about his business as a masonry and concrete contractor. Often, he would meet his workers at the brewery on Fridays and pay them as he sat having his golden ales. He would also tell me about his three daughters: their names, their ages, where they went to school, and where they worked. On occasion, he would bring one or two of them to eat dinner.

Again, I was being lured away from my marriage and my family. Satan was using every trick in the book, and I was following with eager abandon. Although I was going to church while all of this was happening, my very immature understanding of God did not protect me or prevent me from following my fleshly desires, wants, and needs. I yearned for a way out of my marriage, and I didn't know at the time, but this friend—this man—was going to be that for me. After a few more weeks of small talk, I asked him out. I said we should go out for drinks sometime. He said he would love to. He asked for my number, and I gave it to him without hesitating. A few days passed, and no call, no invitation, no text, nothing. The next time I saw him at the brewery, he told me he called and some guy answered. He was sure I had given him the wrong number. I asked him to show me the number I had given him on his phone. When he did, it was mine. I assured him it was my number. He responded, "Oh look, I put you in my phone right below Hyme, a guy who works for me. I must have accidentally called him instead."

We laughed at that, and he asked what day I wanted to have breakfast with him. I picked February 28, 2006, a day that Mark was out of town working and the boys would be in school. We decided on a restaurant downtown on Main Street. This guy had never seen me outside the brewery, where I was always working. He had only seen me in jeans, my work t-shirt, my waitress apron, and my hair in a ponytail or a bun on top of my head. I made sure I looked my best for our date, so I wore my hair down with natural curls, and I put on jeans and a light blue ribbed turtleneck sweater. When our table was ready, we were escorted to a booth towards the back of the restaurant. We sat across from each other and read over the menus. The waitress took our order, and as we ate, a conversation started that would change our lives.

Even though this was a date, it didn't feel like one. It was like I was sitting with and talking to an old friend, playing catch up after not seeing each other for many years. It was comfortable and relaxed, and talking flowed easily for both of us. The first question he asked me was, "What are your beliefs about God?"

I told him I had been baptized at nine years old, believed in God, Jesus, and the Holy Spirit, and attended a local church most Sundays. Of course, I left out what my walk (or lack thereof) with God looked like all those years. He said, "Good, now we can continue."

He didn't waste any time and was very upfront about his past. I learned he had used drugs and been addicted to methamphetamines, had been to jail and prison, had been married two times before, and was currently going through a third divorce. He also shared more about his children and a little about his upbringing. He said it was important I knew the truth about him, so if anything he was sharing was too much for me to handle, he wanted to know now, and we could be friends and not pursue a romantic relationship.

I shared a little about myself—some of the real me but mostly the same old half-truths, lies, and exaggerations I had shared most of my adult life. I was having breakfast with someone sharing some pretty intimate, colored details about his life, being open and honest, and in my mind, I still could not get myself to tell the truth. I was afraid he would not like the real me and not want to date me. One of the lies I spewed that morning was that Mark and I were in the process of getting a divorce. I told him we still lived together but were not married as a couple. The reality was my husband had no idea that I wanted to leave him and that I was looking for a way out.

After we finished breakfast, we strolled downtown, out in the open, as if I had nothing to hide. Was I subconsciously trying to get caught? What if someone saw me and called my husband? It was time for me to pick up James at preschool, so we parted ways in the parking lot. We hugged each other quickly, talked about seeing each other soon at the brewery, got in our cars, and parted ways. I enjoyed myself with him and was sure God sent him to me since he was a believer. I was telling myself how great it would be to have a godly man to help me raise the boys. I was so delusional!

Not long after our first date, we went out to a local Mexican restaurant. We sat at the bar, sharing a "fishbowl margarita" as we lovingly called it. Who knows how much tequila was in that one drink, but we sat there, flirting, talking, and learning more about each other, our pasts, our likes, and our dislikes. After what must have been two hours or so, we decided it was time to head out. Instead of saying goodbye, we ended up in the front seat of his truck, sharing our first kiss. It was passionate and powerful and everything I wanted to feel. We sat there for hours kissing, touching, and making out like teenagers under the bleachers at the high school stadium.

I was unsure where this relationship was going, but I wanted to find out. We would meet, talk, learn more about each other, go on hikes and long car rides, and make out. We eventually went all the way. In my mind, there was no turning back, and I was sure I was in love with Kenny. He quickly learned I was not as close to a divorce as I had led on. He even tried to break it off, telling me he could not do this because he felt guilty. I told him I understood but wanted him to know he was my Kenny in shining armor, sent by God to rescue me and my boys from my misery. After some thought, he said he wanted to continue dating me and see where it was going. Our relationship was official—well, official to us. We both pulled love goggles on to keep away the glare of the red flags each of us was waving in plain sight. Blinded by Satan's deceptions, we ignored what should have sent each of us running as fast as we could have in opposite directions.

CHAPTER 18

Confessing My Unfaithfulness

It was late spring of 2006 when Mark found some texts on my phone from one of my male friends from the brewery. He did a little digging, called some of the numbers on our cell phone bill, and asked the guys on the other end how they knew me. He texted me at work that he needed to talk about things he found on my phone. I was sure he had learned about Kenny. I asked to go home early from work. The boys were not there when I arrived, so we talked. Now was my chance, to be honest and confess I was having an affair. I do not know how I brought myself to say the words, but I confessed to him I was cheating on him with a man I met at the brewery.

I will never forget the look on Mark's face. He was crying, mad, and so angry. He went outside and cursed and threw things. After a few tense minutes, he came back inside and asked me some tough questions. Here and now, I was more honest than ever with him. I told him there had been other instances of infidelity throughout our marriage. I hurt him so badly. But part of me wanted to. I wanted him to hurt like I had hurt all those years and was never able to express. He screamed for me to get out. I packed some clothes and returned to my new home away from home, the brewery. I told a co-worker what had happened, and she offered to let me stay with her for a bit.

Immediately, my husband contacted his brother, an Arizona lawyer. He suggested that he remove me from the bank accounts and do what he could to protect himself, at least financially. Weirdly, I was okay with all the demands he was making of me. I didn't want to be tied to him in any way. This was my escape plan. After a few days, Mark and I discussed the logistics of navigating what was happening and what would happen in our relationship. We decided when he was on duty, I would stay at the house with the boys, and when he was home, I would stay with my friend from work. He asked me if I would go to counseling, and I agreed. He did not want to go to couples therapy but rather to individual counseling. He was sure something was wrong with me for what I had done to him and our marriage. I went for a few weeks until I convinced myself that Kenny was who I wanted to be with.

After it was apparent that we were not going to heal or repair our marriage, Mark filed for divorce. We wanted to be as civil as possible with each other and keep it out of court, so we used a divorce mediator to help us split up our stuff and decide who got what—the house, the cars, the debt. We also discussed child custody and spousal support. I declined spousal support and forfeited my rights to any of his future retirement, partly because I was trying to be nice and to cut as many ties to him as I could, but also out of guilt and shame.

Because of finances, I couldn't move out into my own place until later that year. We did our best in those months leading up to the eventual splitting of the home to make life for us and the boys feel as "normal" as possible. We wanted to ensure we did the best we could to make their new reality as easy as possible. We took our boys to a counselor, or as we called it for them, the "feelings doctor." We didn't do everything perfectly, but we were on the same page about protecting the boys as much as we could.

Mark struggled, as expected, with me being in a relationship with Kenny, and he requested I not bring him around the boys or be allowed in our home. His main concern was Kenny's past. He was sure he was not a good role model for the boys and might somehow harm them. I know Mark spoke and acted out of anger, hurt, and pain. Because of my recent confessions, he was sure Kenny was only the start of many men I would have relationships with. He wanted me to keep all of them away from the boys.

CHAPTER 19

Adjusting To The Differences

O nce I moved out of the house in August 2006, having my own place with the boys was a blast. We set up the house the way I wanted to, had a schedule that worked for me and the boys, ate the food we wanted to, and had friends over when we wanted to. The custody arrangement with my ex was always based on his work calendar with the fire department. I would arrange the calendar so he could work a few days in a row, and when he was off, he would have the boys. When he was working, I had them. So it was different week to week, month to month. Sometimes, I had the boys for four days, then their father would have them for five, then back to me for three, then at his house for six, and then at mine for five. Back and forth, back and forth. We had 50/50 custody, so we made sure that each of us had a perfect split of days for the month.

This wasn't always easy for the boys or us adults, but we did not want either parent or child to feel like they were not wanted. Most of the time we made decisions about the boys together, like doctors' appointments, medical procedures, school, clothes, finances, etc. The challenges came because there were different rules, expectations, and discipline at each house. At my place, we had boundaries and rules that fit our moral beliefs. My ex was more laid back. He dealt with issues as they arose, and because he isn't a believer, what he thought was acceptable differed from what I believed. There was also the difference in incomes between the two houses. My ex had extra money he could spend on the boys that I could not. This created a feeling that "Dad's house is where we have all the fun" and "Mom's house is the rules, homework, and chores house." Kenny and I referred to Mark as "Disneyland Dad."

Another area of parenting differences that became apparent was my ex trying to be buddies with the boys. It was like they were three college students living together in a frat house watching whatever TV they wanted to, staying up as late as they wanted, and eating whatever they wanted. Now that the boys are older, I've learned that sneaking out until all hours of the night was not uncommon, especially for James. He told me how as early as fifth or sixth grade, he would sneak out, venture miles away from home, sneak back in at two or three am, and get ready for school without having slept at all.

I was always trying to make things easier on my ex-husband. Why? I am sure it was out of guilt. I believed I deserved any inconvenience and discomfort I was feeling. I gave him priority for scheduling, drove the boys to him on many occasions, and canceled my plans if his schedule changed. Even when I moved over a half hour away from the boys' school, I drove them back and forth each day. I believed having the boys stay at the school they knew with their friends was essential to their emotional health. Maybe it was, or perhaps it didn't matter. The root of all my giving in to whatever my ex wanted was because I was sure I owed him after what I had done in our marriage.

Reflection Questions For Section 3

1. What people, places or things have you run to in order to feel important, accepted, secure and fulfilled? Have those things ever disappointed you? Is it hard for you to believe and trust God can and always will be able to meet these deep needs? Reflect on what Philippians 4:19 means to you. "And my God will supply all your needs according to his riches in glory in Christ Jesus."

2. Have you ever experienced pain and betrayal in a relationship from porn use? Do you consider porn as a form of adultery? Read Matthew 5:28 "But I tell you, everyone who looks at a woman lustfully has already committed adultery with her in his heart." What does lust mean to you? What do you think Jesus was saying in this scripture?

3. Reflect on the devastation that can be caused from committing adultery. What factors may have contributed to strain and eventually infidelity in your relationship or marriage? How have you navigated these challenges? What factors can or has contributed to rebuilding trust, healing and restoration in your relationship or

marriage? How can surrendering the guilt and shame of this betrayal to God lead to healing and restoration? What steps can you take to surrender the brokenness and pain of infidelity to God? Did you or will you seek help from a Christian marriage counselor or coach?

4. Have you ever felt isolated or alone, even if you are in a relationship? What did you do to try and feel connected? Read Deuteronomy 31:6 "Be strong and courageous; don't be terrified or afraid of them. For the Lord your God is the one who will go with you; he will not leave you or abandon you." and Matthew 8:28b "And remember, I am with you always, to the end of the age." Can you find comfort in this scripture knowing that God will never leave you or forsake you? Even if people fail us, disappoint us, or abandon us or reject us, God never will!

5. How does prayer and seeking wisdom and guidance from Jesus and the Scriptures impact and strengthen your relationship or marriage? How can surrendering to God's plan for motherhood and marriage bring about peace and fulfilment in these roles?

SECTION 4

A NEW HUSBAND & MORE DYSFUNCTION

"For where your treasure lies, there your heart will be also."

Matthew 6:21(CSB)

CHAPTER 20

Looking Through Love Goggles

Even though I was thrilled to have a man to worship Jesus with, Kenny and I were going to church when it fit into our schedule. We put our relationship with God on an "as we need Him basis." Well, at least I did. Kenny was in the Word every day. He liked to say, "A verse a day keeps the devil away." When we attended church, we would come in, praise God, sing songs, listen to the sermon, and talk a little about how good it was. All the while, we were living in sin: not married, sometimes neglecting our children, spending money whenever and wherever we wanted, drinking, and not paying attention to Kenny's business. These were just a few of the ways we were not putting God first in our lives. Despite how fantastic life together felt, things started to unravel. Cracks in the relationship began to bleed out. Money was tight, the business experienced hardships, the boys were struggling in their own ways, and Kenny'' daughters were making choices that would affect the rest of their lives. God was trying to get our attention.

In February 2007, Kenny and I moved in together. Shortly after, he proposed to me at one of our favorite restaurants. We decided it would be unique to get married on the anniversary of our first date, which was February 28. We prepared to have forty-five people attend the wedding, including our children, family, and a few close friends. The venue owners made it so that we could have the ceremony right there in the restaurant. The reception would be a sit-down meal with a choice of entrée and beverages for the guests. We kept the decorations to a few hydrangeas and blue accent candies on the tables. The building itself is so beautiful. At one time in history, it was a Pony Express stop for the mail. Of course, it still had most of the original brick, and as a masonry contractor, Kenny loved it. There was no need to decorate since it was romantic and beautiful. There were no flower girls or ring bearers, no groomsmen or bridesmaids. My boys walked me down the aisle, which was situated perfectly between the dinner tables. One of Kenny's best friends, Pastor Earl, married us.

We only had a little extra money, so our wedding budget was tight. We kept costs down by deciding not to pay a fancy photographer to take pictures. Most people had cell phones, and with the disposable cameras, we were sure we would get enough images to enjoy. It turned out a client Kenny was in the process of building some fireplaces for, was an excellent wedding photographer. She loved the work Kenny was doing for her, and she was so excited for us that as a gift, she photographed our wedding for us for free! It was such a blessing.

Kenny's daughters helped me pick out my wedding dress at a local shop. He had a beautiful blue suit jacket, and he wore it with his cream kakis, which matched the color of my dress. The boys wore what boys wear: pants and dress shirts. The girls and I had fun shopping for matching dresses and shoes for them to wear. Each of their dresses were the same color but was a style that fit their personality. It was a magical day for us all. We wrote our vows, celebrated with those who attended, and promised there in front of God and all who heard that we were in this for the long haul.

Not long after we came home from the honeymoon, the mud hit the fan! I was getting glimpses of Kenny's anger for the first time. With all the pressure from his business and the economic downturn, money was not flowing in for him like it had in the previous years. On top of that, we were awarded a win in a lawsuit brought against Kenny and his company, but we were left owing legal fees for both sides that were well over one hundred thousand dollars.

We struggled to make ends meet and decided to let the house go back to the bank. We declared bankruptcy to get out of all the debt and legal fees.

Despite all the turmoil and devastation of bankruptcy, we felt a sense of renewal in our lives after it was all said and done. At this time, we were still living with our love goggles on. Both of us were ignoring the red flags that were waving in our faces since the day we met: my insecurities, low self-esteem, fears of abandonment and rejection, dishonesty, and trying to get my needs met from people and things. Plus there was Kenny's anger, temper, drinking, lying, fear of being cheated on, jealousy and mistrust issues. These are just a few pieces of the baggage we brought with us into the marriage. Neither of us wanted to give our junk to God, and the flimsy emotional zippers could not hold the contents in forever. Eventually, all those issues just exploded all over our lives.

Along with my U-Haul and his semi-truck full of issues, we each brought expectations of what marriage should look and feel like. Kenny's expectations were more traditional, like "I want to have sex" and "I want you to clean and cook and keep the house looking nice." His big ones were not to lie to or cheat on him and to always respect him. My expectations were less tangible: if you loved me, you would know what I want without me having to ask; you will make me whole, you will plug the holes in my heart, and you will love me, accept me, desire me, make me feel secure, and never leave me. In pre-marital class, we never talked about these issues or learned how they would affect our marriage, our children, our family, or, especially, our walk with God.

CHAPTER 21

If I Can Just Fix Him

In 2008, the economy took a nosedive, and many people were not opting to add extras like a custom outdoor fireplace or backyard barbeque. Kenny's business took a hit. Jobs were still trickling in but not like before. Money became tight, and neither of us was trusting in God like we should have been during these hard financial times—not because we were making a conscious choice not to but rather because we did not know how to live a financially biblical way.

I am sure God used the stress in our lives to allow the issues to start popping out of our emotional baggage. Kenny started drinking more and more. He was often drunk before coming home to the beer or wine in the fridge. I was clueless that he would stop at the store and drink a six-pack on his way home or spend a few hours drinking at the brewery. When he was intoxicated, he would become a different person. Things I said or did in the past would irritate him, and he would bring up my offenses from months earlier. Most of the time, it was a jealousy issue or because some guy looked at me this way or that way or someone had made a comment to me that Kenny thought was inappropriate. His anger was because he thought I did not handle it correctly or I was hiding something from him, lying to him, or maybe even cheating on him with this person. I did lie—not about what was happening in the here and now but about the things that had happened in my past. I convinced myself at the time I was saving him from being upset, but it was about alleviating my fears. If Kenny knew what I had done in my past, he would reject me and leave me, like I believed everyone else had done.

As the year went on, there were a few incidents when he would be drunk, get upset, and then leave. That was another one of his MOs. When things got heated or tense, he would leave. I do not mean walk out for good, but he would be gone for days. He wouldn't even answer his phone. This would send me into a panic. As he headed out, I would chase him, begging him not to go, asking him to talk to me. "Can I explain? Can I tell you my side?" I tried to appease him, telling him what I thought he wanted to hear to help him not leave. What he wanted was the truth, but I just could not say it. I was too afraid.

While Kenny was gone, I would replay what had happened over and over in my head. I would pray and ask God to please bring him home. I would negotiate with God, promising I would fill-in-the-blank if he would bring my husband home. During the days Kenny was absent, I was a wreck. I couldn't eat or sleep. I was a walking zombie. I felt hopeless, and a deep despair that I was sure had no end settled over me. I was convinced he was never coming home, that I was going to end up divorced and alone again. I was sure that all of this was my fault, that I was not good enough, and that I was not worth anyone loving me. Somehow, I deserved all this for the bad things I had done in my life. God must be punishing me for cheating on my ex-husband.

Most of the time, after Kenny had a few days to cool down, he came back. We would try and talk to resolve what had happened, but we never talked about the root cause. We didn't even know there was a root cause to talk about. We believed what happened was from some present action or situation between us. We had no idea there were deep origins of dysfunction pulling us down. We had no concept that the different bits of baggage from our pasts were colliding against each other, spewing contents all over our relationship.

In November 2008, I started to understand that Kenny's drinking played a significant role in his anger and our blowups. I was sure I could fix him and lead him to stop drinking, and this would make everything better. All I needed to do was find a good book or someone to help us. We were attending church more regularly now because we had more time. This did not mean we put God first in our lives or marriage. We were not attending any Bible study or small groups; we would only go Sunday morning and pretend we were right with God and each other. At the church I learned they had a group called Celebrate Recovery. One Thursday night, I went by myself. I was going to learn about how I could fix Kenny's drinking and get him to stop.

But at that first meeting I learned the exact opposite. They explained I could not make him do anything; he had to want it for himself. They did introduce me to the concept of being co-dependent on Kenny. What? Do you mean I have a part to play in this? You mean I need to change, and when I change this will help him? I was told it was no accident I was there, and God had some work to do in me. God wanted me to remove the plank in my eye like Jesus talks about in Matthew 7:3. I needed to worry about healing myself and removing my own bad habits before I could point to any sin or issues Kenny had. I thought, *Okay, fix me fast so I can move on to him!* I let Kenny know about my experience at Celebrate Recovery and explained I would be going to help me so I could help him. But he was not ready to give up the drinking yet, and after a few weeks, I stopped going. I, too, was not prepared for true healing. The reality was I was convinced if Kenny stopped drinking, all of our problems would disappear, we would live happily ever after, and I would have the marriage I always dreamed about.

On New Year's Eve, Kenny and I had a few friends over. We ate, drank, and watched fireworks from our yard. Kenny had more to drink than usual, and the night ended badly. He had been upset about something I did or didn't do for weeks, and of course, now was the perfect time to bring it up. It became an argument, and our typical pattern ensued. He was mad. I chased and tried to make him feel better, but the more I chased, the angrier he got. Eventually he left and ghosted me. I was miserable and worried. He stayed away for a few days, then came home, and slowly warmed back up. We made up and went back to our everyday lives. I was so tired of this routine, and I knew Kenny needed help that I could not provide him. I contacted a friend of Kenny's who ran a rehabilitation house for men. I asked him to call Kenny and give him the help he needed. This friend told me that he was sorry but until Kenny wanted help and reached a point where he was willing to change, there was nothing anyone could do for him. Kenny had to want to stop drinking for himself.

This is not what I wanted to hear! I was devastated, but I knew I could not live like this. I would not raise my boys around this, period. They had only witnessed a few of Kenny's anger episodes, and it was by God's grace they were always at their dad's or somewhere else when we had our dysfunctional cycle. I somehow got up the courage to tell Kenny I would not be able to continue like this anymore, and he needed to find help. All I could do now was pray. So I prayed and prayed and prayed. Nothing happened then, but God had a plan, and on January 19, 2009, Kenny went to work as usual, but his day was cut short. He ended up at the brewery at about 10:30 in the morning. He drank and drank. It wasn't much past one or two in the afternoon when he called me, sobbing and saying he had to stop and was going to get some help. He called that friend I mentioned, the one with the rehab for men. When Kenny got home, I remember holding him as we both cried and talked about what the next steps would look like.

Starting January 20, 2009, things began to change. We allowed God the space He needed to start peeling back the layers of sin, dysfunction, pain, shame, and hurt we both had allowed to define us. We attended Celebrate Recovery together, participated in a small group where we worked the steps, and started attending church more regularly. I joined the women's group, and we went back to a Monday night Bible study Kenny was part of years earlier. We did whatever we thought we could to keep Kenny sober. I did not drink in front of him or bring any alcohol home for a few years into his sobriety. His sweet tooth became insatiable after he stopped drinking, so we ate everything covered in chocolate and every kind of ice cream or cake we could get. I wanted to do my part to help him in any way I could. We would worry about the diabetic comas later.

CHAPTER 22

A New Business & More Idols

Work was still slow in 2009, but Kenny got a client who kept him busy most of the year. He created a backyard masterpiece for him with a pizza oven, a BBQ, an outdoor fireplace, walkways, stamped concrete around the pool, and a waterfall. While working for him, Kenny came to find out this guy invested in small companies. One of Kenny's dreams was to get out of producing works of art and start selling the materials to do so. He wanted to take it easier on his body, help homeowners who wanted to do it themselves, and have a place where contractors could shop locally and get most of what they needed in one place. For months, we talked about what this would look like. I researched and came up with the numbers it would take to get it close to running. We prayed about it some, but not like we should have.

In March of 2010, we approached this potential investor. He was interested, so we created a plan to move forward with his financial help. He chose to invest in us, and by late spring, the doors to our masonry, landscape, and concrete supply store were open. At first, we didn't have much product or equipment, but we had each other, and I was all in to help support Kenny's dream. I was alone at the yard in the beginning months while Kenny continued to contract. He would stop in multiple times during the day when he could get away, answer my calls asking for help to understand what a customer wanted, and finish his day with me at the material yard.

These first few months were tough. I was learning things I had no idea I wanted to know. I could maneuver a forklift, use a front-end loader, and back up a ten-wheeler truck, not to mention the millions of different hand tools, materials, and products we were trying to sell. On top of all those things, I had to learn how to set up, run, and keep a retail business afloat. We had to pay employees and file and pay taxes regularly. Then there was everything to do with marketing and advertising, operating costs, accounting software, retail inventory software, markups, and profits and margins. I was getting my MBA on the spot in real time.

After that first winter, we knew we had to gear up and bring in as many materials as possible. Kenny was working double time, and so was I. When he wasn't at the yard, I was doing the work of three people. I was getting tired and resentful. This material yard was not my dream; it was Kenny's. Although I was excited to help him achieve it, I did not grow up telling myself all I ever wanted to do was drive a front-end loader and load customers' cars with mulch, gravel, or whatever they needed. I approached Kenny, telling him now was when I needed him to be all in or else this wouldn't work.

He agreed, and in the spring of 2011, Kenny was working full-time alongside me. We were able to hire an employee to help in the yard because one of Kenny's main jobs was driving the transfer truck to deliver goods to customers and pick up supplies from distributors. It was an exciting time. But it was also some of the most stressful, tiring days of our lives. We were at the yard by 6 am, and we closed and made it home by 6 pm—all while still having the two boys we were helping to raise.

Those years were tough, especially on James. He has since told me he hated our material yard because it took his mom away from him. Looking back, it was all-consuming. We poured ourselves into it with abandon. We did what we could for the boys to have fun, but working full-time six days a week left little time and energy to love on them. Our children were not the only ones to suffer. We only had time for God by glancing at His Word in the morning or when we could fit Him into our schedule. Sometimes, we would go to a church service after work on Saturday to sleep in and do all that was needed at the house on Sunday. We sure did not have time to attend small groups or fellowship with other believers. God was not first in our lives or our marriage, and we were not showing our children how to put Him first either.

Diamond Central Building Materials had become our idol. We were looking for it to fulfill us, tell us who we were, and make us feel accepted and loved by others through our accomplishments. The business was our security, but God was about to flip our world upside down so that we would get our priorities straight. He would show us that it wasn't really Him we were worshipping.

At the beginning of 2015, we were up to our eyeballs in business bills. We owed people money, and there was no way to stock up for the spring. To make matters worse, we had to replace all three delivery trucks with smog-compliant ones. We could only handle these issues if we used our house for collateral. Kenny and I thought about it, and we decided there was no way we would leverage what we perceived as our only security in life. So before the spring even started, we had a closing sale. We sold everything we could, returned merchandise to those vendors who would take it back, and filed another bankruptcy.

We were confused, upset, and disappointed with what was happening to us. We asked ourselves why God would allow the business to fail and crumble before our eyes. We believed God had opened the doors for our company, and we thought He had orchestrated meeting the investor, pointed us in the direction of the property owners, and provided money, materials, employees, and customers. We were working our tails off, and learning all we could about running a retail business. We put all we had physically, emotionally, and mentally into this business. We had looked to everyone and everything to give us wisdom and advice—everyone, that is, except God.

CHAPTER 23

Porn, The Other Woman

When Kenny and I first got together, I was intentional about telling him how porn was a big no-no in my life. I would not tolerate it in our home or anywhere in our relationship. He understood the deep scars it had made in my heart. Porn represented trauma I had not turned over to God or allowed Him to heal in me. So Kenny knew how important it was to me to keep pornography far away from our marriage. When we started our material company, it was just about when the smartphone was making its surge. Right in the palm of your hand, you had the internet, and with that, you had access to the good, the bad, and the ugly. I am not exactly sure how or when Kenny discovered porn on his phone, but he was tempted and fell prey to Satan's ways. Kenny tells me he would use porn for a while and then be so convicted. He would feel dirty and shameful, and he would pray for forgiveness and make vows and promises to stop using it. This became a pattern for him.

I suspected Kenny was watching porn, but instead of confronting him and asking him about it, I would sneak around like an undercover spy, looking for evidence. I would snoop on his phone and browse the internet history on all his devices. When he was in the shower, I would look at his Facebook page and texts. I was determined to catch him. Sure, I wanted to know what I felt was right, but even if I found something, what would I really do? I hated confrontation, and this was such a touchy subject for me. It was painful to think he knew how damaging pornography was in my life as a child and in my last marriage. How could he do this to me? To us?

Kenny became a master at hiding his sin. Most of us are. I do not know if you have ever been part of a relationship where porn is an issue. It may surprise you how most spouses react to finding out their significant other is using porn. There may be an initial confirmation or declaration of disgust from the wounded partner, but usually, it is dealt with in the dark. For me, I was sure there was something wrong with me. Why would he need to use porn? Wasn't I enough? Was I fat or ugly? Did I have the wrong hair color? Were my boobs, legs, butt, or face not what he wanted? I experienced shame and embarrassment, which heightened my insecurities about myself. I felt so rejected. Satan used the wounds I had deep down inside to keep me further separated from God and Kenny. I was trying to get my acceptance, identity, and security from my husband instead of God. So when Kenny used porn, I believed not only was he failing me as a husband, but I also must be failing him as a wife. I internalized and personalized his sin. During these years, I could never tell Kenny how I was feeling. If I confronted him, he would tell me the truth—that I was not enough—and he would leave. So I stuffed my feelings out of fear.

CHAPTER 24

Now Do I Have Your Attention

Kenny was now back to work as a masonry and concrete contractor, and his body was reminding him of all the places that were wearing out. For years, he struggled with a big toe that had at one point been broken in his early 20s and now had arthritis. We consulted an orthopedic doctor, and after trying anti-inflammatory meds, cortisone shots, shoe inserts, ice, and more ice, it was apparent that Kenny's only choice was to have surgery to correct it. So in December 2015 he had his big toe fused. He had to be off of it for at least six weeks. The timing was perfect because he usually did not work during the winter months. By spring, Kenny was back to normal, and our lives and marriage felt on track.

All the while, we each were struggling internally with our sin, not completely surrendering ourselves to God or putting Him first in our marriage. We gave it excellent lip service, though. We showed up to church on Sundays and went to our small group Bible study. Again, we were fitting Jesus into our lives, not having our lives fit in after we filled up or gave our best to God. Then, one day, God decided to get our attention once again. Have you ever been on the receiving end of a God-orchestrated event where He is trying to get your attention? Often, it is not fun, pleasant, or without pain.

God was about to rock our world to get us to put down our idols, get rid of sin, and unpack more of the baggage we had never surrendered. Two days before we were supposed to leave for a six-week vacation, Kenny made his way to a last-minute doctor's appointment for a cortisone shot in his shoulder. I was sitting at my sewing machine, creating a light jacket to bring with me on vacation. Kenny called after his doctor's appointment to ask if I needed anything from the store. I assured him I was all good, and he told me he was on his way and I would see him soon. Next thing you know, I got a cryptic text from Kenny telling me he was at the fire station. I was curious why he would stop there, so I tried to call him, but he did not answer me. I went into panic mode thinking I had upset him somehow. I was worried it was the start of one of our conflict cycles.

This time, someone else answered. It was one of the firefighters. He informed me that Kenny was there, being assessed. They had called Life Flight and were going to transport him via air ambulance to Roseville Medical Center. *What?! Why?* The young man told me that they believed Kenny was having a cardiac emergency. They were waiting for an ambulance to hook him up to a twelve lead to tell them exactly what was wrong, but his symptoms were presenting as a heart issue. I said I would be right over. I headed to the fire station, which was only a few minutes from our house. I was in panic mode, crying out to God, saying "Please, Jesus. Please, Jesus. Please, Jesus." When I got to the fire station, they had moved Kenny to the front seat of the rescue truck, preparing to drive him to the airstrip to transport him by helicopter. Because of my education and having my EMT, I was able to see the strip of paper with his EKG results on it. He looked to be blocked in a part of his heart. I was able to hold his hand as they prepared to fly him off. He told me he was scared. I assured him he would be okay, and I promised to be there when he landed.

I called Kenny's three daughters, and I made sure my ex could grab James from school. I was not able to drive because I was so worried. The fire chief drove me into town, where Ashley (Kenny's oldest daughter) was waiting for me. I jumped into her car, and she drove us to Roseville, a thirty-five-minute drive from where she picked me up. All we could do was ask each other what had just happened and why it happened, and we were convincing ourselves he would be okay. When we arrived, she dropped me off at the ER entrance. I ran to the receptionist, who buzzed me in the back to find Kenny. It turns out he was not in the cubicle where they said but instead had been rushed to the OR for surgery. I was escorted back to a waiting room, where Madison and Valarie (Kenny's other two daughters) were waiting for us. Within minutes of Ashley joining us, the nurse returned and asked for me. I was escorted into the hall, where they were wheeling Kenny out on his way to the ICU.

The surgeon explained that Kenny had a blockage in his LAD artery, which supplies blood to the front of the left side of the heart. He said he was in surgery when Kenny arrived via helicopter and stopped the quadruple bypass he was performing to save Kenny's life. He further explained that this type of blockage is known as the widow maker because only 3 to 7 percent of patients survive the event. Kenny never lost consciousness and only went into cardiac arrest as the doctor was placing the stent in this major artery in his heart. The doctor told us Kenny went over forty-five minutes without properly oxygenated blood going to the back of his heart, and we would not know the extent of the damage for a few days. I heard everything the doctor was telling me, but it wasn't computing like it should have. It had not sunk in, and I could only ask, "We have a six-week trip planned to the East Coast, and we are leaving in two days. Can he still go?"

The surgeon and nurses must have thought I was an idiot. But at that moment, I was not fully aware of the implications of what had just happened. The doctor said, "No, you better cancel the trip. He cannot fly for a while and will be hospitalized for a few days." Right after hearing those words, I—Heidi, the organized, hyper-focused learner—stepped out and went to work. I had many phone calls and emails to send to cancel flights, Airbnb stays, excursions, tours, and hotel rooms. I had to call friends and family.

Here we were, facing one of the biggest trials of our lives. I was praying and asking God to help, but I was leading and not following God's way. I was trying to take control because control makes me feel secure and safe. I like to do whatever I can to ease my tension and fear by being in charge. I am unsure if this is because I believe I'm the only one I can count on in my situation or because I finally feel like I can handle the things I wish I could have as a child.

Those first few days while I was in the ICU with Kenny, I was reading and researching all I could about heart disease, the widow maker, diet, exercise, and how to fix Kenny's heart. I promised Kenny I would do what I do best: researching and learning all I could to help him recover fully. Here I was again, using a time of distress to immerse and distract myself from the fear and anxiety I was having by diving deep into my strength as a learner. Why was I not running to God? Why was I not holding Kenny's hand and praying? Why was I relying on Heidi and what I thought was best? Why was I not trusting God and His ways, timing, and pace?

Kenny spent five days in ICU and two days in acute care before they released him to go home. I stayed in a hotel room in the area for four days, and then I was allowed to stay with him in his room for those last two days. Before we left, his heart function (the power, strength, and amount his heart was working) was 35 percent. Yes, that is low, and for a few days after the event, his heart was functioning only at 33 percent, and they were considering putting him on the transplant list. It was a touchy few days.

When we left the hospital, we took a grocery bag full of meds. There were so many I had to make a chart and use one of those pill-sorting containers to keep it all straight. We decided to adopt a vegan diet together. This was going to be rough for my meat-and-potatoes guy. I bought every book I could find on food, nutrition, and recovering from heart disease. After a few days, we met with a local cardiologist. He explained more about Kenny's condition and prognosis and what he believed would be the best path for Kenny to take. It included the bag of medicine he was sent home with, with a few minor tweaks for brands and doses. The doctors in the hospital and this cardiologist all kept telling us the regimen they had him on was typical for a post-stent placement heart patient. They knew what they were doing, right? The doctors kept treating Kenny like all their other patients. But why was this especially irritating to me? When I asked about their typical patient, it was a 73-year-old man, not a 54-year-old man with low blood pressure, cholesterol under two hundred, and a physically fit body.

By October of the following year, Kenny struggled to lift a ninety four-pound bag of cement. He was having reactions and side effects from many of his medications. His heart function was now only about 37 percent, and his cholesterol shot up to three hundred. Why was all of this happening if we were following the doctors' instructions? Well, we realized that Kenny is sensitive to legumes, so eating a vegan diet of beans, chickpeas, and pea protein sent his body into protection mode. His liver would release cholesterol, thinking his body was under attack. Plus, the meds were causing Kenny to have vertigo, motion sickness, and low blood pressure, and they were robbing his body of crucial nutrients and vitamins for muscle function.

We were both done listening to what the doctors told us, and after lots of research, we decided to gain back muscle and heart function. We treated Kenny's heart and body like bodybuilders do. We put him on supplements like L-carnitine, D-ribose, vitamin E, garlic, and magnesium, to name a few. We started eating lean meats and stopped all the legumes. We weaned him off a few of the medications that we had incorporated as supplements. Within weeks, Kenny was feeling better. His strength was coming back. New blood work showed that his cholesterol returned closer to what it was pre-heart event. The doctor ordered a stress test and an echocardiogram to measure heart function, which was now at 47 percent. To anyone who would listen, we would say that God's hand was all over Kenny's heart event, that it wasn't his time to go, and that God saved him for some reason. With our mouths, we were confessing God as Lord, but our lives showed He was still not in first place.

CHAPTER 25

More Distractions From Our Dysfunction

I n the spring, Kenny was healthy enough to start working again. I also started looking at ways to bring in extra money to help alleviate the financial burden off Kenny's shoulders. With the skills I acquired over the years working at our material yard and doing the books for Kenny's business, I thought I could start my own business as a bookkeeper. That sounded right up my alley. I started preparing a name, logo, systems, procedures, pricing, advertising, and all the startup stuff. I would specialize in bookkeeping, system setup, procedure creation, and safety manual implementation for contractors.

As I was launching my business, someone from a prominent local engineering company contacted me and asked if I would like to interview for a position with them. I talked to Kenny about it, and we decided it wouldn't hurt for me to take the interview. They made me an offer that was too good to pass up, so I accepted it. This would mean my bookkeeping business would not happen, but I would be guaranteed a steady paycheck, health benefits, and a retirement package. The pay was good too. It differed from what I could have done with my own business, but it offered less risk and more consistency.

I was one of only a handful of women in this male-dominated business. I had to interact and work closely with men in my everyday duties. Most of the men in these positions were married with children. All of them were very friendly, and we had a good working relationship. But even though these men were mainly professionals, there were times they said and did things that not necessarily appropriate to say and do in front of women. They would try to push the acceptable boundaries with off-color jokes or comments about their wives or girlfriends, and then they'd wait to see how I would respond. Of course, I wanted everyone to like me, so I pretended to be one of the guys, and I would laugh or joke back. It was fun to be included, even if it meant accepting the foul language or participating in it myself.

There was one man in the office who was in a dating relationship. He would joke along with the other guys and then go a little further. He started telling me things about his girlfriend and their dating life. He would confide in me about their issues and ask for my help in solving his problems. I did not think answering him, joking with him, or talking about his personal life was a bad thing. I thought this was just a co-worker/friend I was helping. It felt good that someone was listening to me, paying attention to me, complimenting me, and making me feel useful. I should have been getting those needs filled from God or my husband, not this man.

Despite God's attempt to bring us to our knees and to Him, we were still struggling with our sins. I was not feeling loved the way I believed I should. One way I eased the pain was by shopping. The cost of the thing I was buying didn't matter. Hunting for deals and browsing for hours sidetracked my mind from remembering that I was hurting. It was always a temporary rush. Then I would feel guilty for spending money. I would lie about how much I spent and sometimes hide what I bought because I was afraid of Kenny's reaction. Yes, I knew this was not what I should be doing, but when I was *shopping*, nothing else seemed to matter. The sin of secrecy was temporary relief, though it could not do for me what I wanted it to do: make me feel loved and accepted no matter who I was in my past or who I was in that moment.

For his part, Kenny used work to meet his needs. And when what he had in his business started not being enough, he wanted more—not just money but more significance. So Kenny started looking for, creating, and coming up with new ways, plans, and ideas to help him fill the void. One such way presented itself through a friend of his. It was doing something Kenny had always been passionate about: gold recovery. This friend built a special machine to dredge gold from the Bering Sea in Alaska. Kenny was so excited about this expedition that he spent hours helping his friend develop and test the machine.

This friend ended up inviting Kenny to go to Nome, Alaska with him. He brought the idea home and explained all the ins and outs to me. Before he even "asked," though, he had already decided he was going, no matter what I said. Kenny explained to me that this was a once-in-a-lifetime opportunity. He had always been into gold recovery; it was a sure thing, and he would come home with tons of gold that would change our lives. I was not sure how this was such a sure thing, but I was told that the gold recovered should be substantial based on the testing of the ocean floor they would be mining in. I was not happy with the idea at all. How was I going to live without him for four months?

I started to stress that once Kenny was there, he would become rich and no longer want or need me. What about the women there? Would he cheat on me, fall in love with another woman, and leave me for her? How would he go four months without being physical with me or anyone? Would he start watching porn again? I was afraid of all these things, and I did not want him to go. But I was afraid to express my feelings out in case Kenny would not like what he heard and run the other way. It did not matter anyway because he made it 100 percent clear that no matter what I thought, he was going. He even used the "I had a heart event and almost died" card.

I put on my pretend attitude and went to work helping him secure flights, luggage, lodging, and special clothes for the cold days and nights—all the things he needed to prepare for the long trip. Being busy with tasks is one way I distract myself from difficult feelings. I chose to stuff them and ensure Kenny was happy and getting what he wanted. After all, I didn't want him upset or mad at me because then he might leave me. Oh wait, that is precisely what he was doing. Sure, not in the "divorce me" kind of leave, but I was not sure it wouldn't end that way. My body was feeling things I did not like, but I was too afraid to express them in a way that worked for Kenny and me.

The time came for Kenny to board his plane and leave for his adventure. There were so many uncertainties in my mind. I liked everything to be in its place and behave like it was supposed to, and I needed to know and control as many details as possible. In this situation, I could not do most of that, so I was more anxious and fearful than usual. It was a strange dynamic in my mind and our relationship at the time.

On the one hand, I trusted Kenny more than I had ever trusted anyone. I loved him more profoundly than I had ever loved anyone. I didn't believe he would hurt me, but I could not be sure. If you had asked me, I would have told you we had a great relationship. So why was I feeling so desperate for him not to leave? I even dreamed at the last minute, he would choose not to go; instead, he would run off the plane, grab me in his arms, and tell me he chose me. Deep down, I believed he was choosing Alaska, gold, his friend, and his desire for money over me and our marriage. And while Kenny was in Alaska, the attention from the man I worked with became even more important to me. At the time, I used it like a drug to numb my pain and fill a void, and once again, I was stepping over the line mentally and emotionally.

Kenny's trip to Alaska turned out differently than he planned or hoped for. The equipment he and his friend had tested out did not work as it should. While Kenny waited for the adjustments and repairs to be made on the machine, he went to work for another miner. Instead of looking for gold, he was doing day labor and getting wages. This was not the windfall Kenny had been hoping for. It was paying his bills while up in Nome, but it needed to replace the income he was losing from his masonry construction business. At least my job was paying for the household bills in his absence. Kenny grew more and more frustrated as the days and weeks went on. He was at week four and had no gold—just labor. I was missing him so much, and he was missing me. We had never been separated this long before. We decided it would be a good time for me to come to Nome. So I requested time off work, got approved for my week away, bought tickets, packed as quickly as possible, and took the sixteen-hour trip on week five of our separation.

I could not get off the plane fast enough when it landed on the runway. I may have been pushing people out of the way as I ran through security to get to the lobby. When I laid eyes on Kenny, it brought butterflies to my stomach and tears to my eyes. I grabbed his face, and we kissed. It wasn't a "Welcome home from work at the end of the day" peck but a hard, long "I am not letting you go" kiss like in the movies. It even received applause and "Ohs" and "Ahs" from those in the lobby. We could not keep our eyes, lips, and hands off each other. Five weeks was too long to be separated. I am pretty sure somewhere in the Bible, God sets a two-week separation limit with a husband and wife. (Or at least He should!) We spent the week reconnecting, traveling, exploring, eating expensive food, and being together mentally, emotionally, physically, and spiritually. We both needed this time to be together in person.

After a few days there, Kenny questioned whether he could or should stay in Nome much longer. He was concerned he would not be making any money other than enough to live on while he was up there. Time was running out, and if he came home now, he could pick up some masonry work in time to put some money away for winter. I assured him it was up to him, although we all know deep down I wanted him home more than I needed air in my lungs. But of course, I was worried that if I spoke my truth, he would be upset, want to stay in Alaska, and never come home.

Not long after talking about it, Kenny made a decision, and I got on the phone to get him a flight home with me on the same plane. I was over the moon. Having him sleep next to me in our king-sized bed was the best feeling in the world. My security, the person whom I relied on to make me feel loved beyond measure, the one whom I wanted approval from more than anyone, was home at last. It made home feel like *home* again.

Kenny was able to jump right back into work. He was getting more and more jobs, and even in the winter he was getting booked for spring. He needed to be gearing up, as we called it, adding more employees to handle the jobs on the books. If this was going to happen, it was going to be hard for me to work outside the house full time, do all my mom tasks, housework, as well as the bookkeeping and accounting for the masonry business. We were bringing in plenty of money now, and Kenny's heart was in great shape, so we decided it would be best for me to leave the engineering company. In spring 2019, I was back to working for us, and it felt great. I loved working from home, supporting Kenny, and doing all I could to help him be successful while still being able to do the things I loved at home. We were back in our groove, doing life according to Kenny and Heidi and fitting God in when it was convenient for us. He was increasingly part of our routine but still not essential in our separate lives or marriage. It was all surface stuff. There was no depth—no genuine relationship.

CHAPTER 26

The Summer of 2019

August of 2019 changed our marriage forever. God still had not gotten our full attention, but He was about to. His plan started with a trip I took to Las Vegas to attend a Def Leppard concert with my longtime friend Marie to celebrate her 49th birthday. She invited me, her business partner, her brother, and two of his friends. There were six of us because that is how many seats there were for a stage-side table. She filled me in on the details and specifics of the trip. I went to Kenny, and we talked about me going. We both have different memories of how this next part went down.

I made arrangements for my flight and booked my room online for the hotel we were all staying in. Over the years, my friend had gifted me with some fantastic, expensive experiences, so paying for her room for the weekend would be special. I remember purposefully withholding this information from Kenny because I was worried he would be upset with me for wanting to spend this extra money. Our group spent two nights in Las Vegas, enjoying good food and drinks, shopping, lying poolside, and the concert. As much as I could, I was texting, calling, and sending pictures to Kenny, filling him in on the details. I was not hiding anything from him other than my plan to pay for my friend's room.

When I got home, Kenny welcomed me, but I could tell something was off. He seemed distant and agitated. My internal alarm bells were going off loudly, making me nervous and anxious, and I was waiting for the bomb to drop. He left for work the next day, and his thoughts, concerns, and fears tortured him. Kenny ruminated all day and all night about what he thought had happened in Las Vegas, and like me, he would not communicate until he couldn't keep it inside any longer. Finally, Kenny exploded. It came out of him like steam escaping from a boiler. He became a different person. His eyes grew dark, he couldn't hear what I was saying, and he hurled foul and abusive words at me. He threw things, punched holes in walls, and kicked over whatever was in his way.

Kenny was sure I had been unfaithful on my trip to Las Vegas, and he was sure I had been seeing someone for a while. He finally confronted me with his fears and suspicions. I denied them. There was no truth to my involvement with anyone in Las Vegas or at home. I had not been with anyone physically other than him since the day we met. I was doing my best to convince him, but he did not believe me. He told me he looked at the room reservation, and it said two occupants on the bill, so he was sure it was confirmation I had brought someone with me or met someone there. I explained that I had nothing to do with what they typed on the bill and that it was their mistake. Then it dawned on me that they marked down two people because I paid for my friend's room.

I admitted to not being honest with Kenny about my plan to pay for my best friend's room. He had difficulty believing this explanation and was upset with me for lying to him. Kenny said if I was lying about something as simple as the money, I could lie about many other things. Of course, he was not just talking about the trip. He knew there were many little things I had lied or withheld the complete truth about over the years, especially about my past. Many of my stories didn't make sense or line up logically to Kenny. So because he knew I lied since the beginning, he believed I was lying now.

Then Kenny brought up something else he was struggling to wrap his mind around. He asked if I was involved with the guy from the engineering company in any way. Had I ever slept with, kissed, or gone out with him? Had he ever been to our house? What did our relationship look like while Kenny was in Alaska? Again, I was defending myself, making excuses for and leaving out things I had said or allowed to be said to me in person and via text. I assured him I was not and had never been interested in the man from the job in that way. Kenny asked me if I had any inappropriate relationship with him, and at that moment, I knew this was my chance to free myself from the guilt and shame of this inappropriate friendship. I revealed to Kenny there had been times when this guy and I had exchanged text messages and had conversations in person where information was exchanged that was inappropriate for a married woman. I admitted to not stopping any of it while working there, but since I left, the contact with him had been minimal.

Kenny was devastated. He asked to see my phone, so I gave it to him. He wanted to see for himself the conversations that took place and if what I told him about my side of the intentions matched with what I had said in the texts. I knew some conversations I had over the years with this man were inappropriate, so I had deleted many of them months earlier and sometimes as they happened. I knew even then that if my husband discovered them, he would lose it and come unglued.

After Kenny read some of the texts, he said he was not sure he could be with me anymore. He did what he had always done when he was mad at me: leave with no communication. I was so scared for my marriage. I was sure it was over, and there was probably nothing I could say to him now to convince him I was not cheating on him. Let's be 100 percent real, though: I was cheating on him. I was having what I might call a mental affair. I was sharing things that should have only been for my husband's ears and mind.

Kenny eventually came home, but he would barely talk to me. He had a rough rest of his day driving, thinking about all that went down between us, and he was even on his way to losing his sobriety. He did not care what happened. He was done and had a "Why bother? Nothing is worth it" attitude in those moments. From his description of what unfolded that afternoon, we are convinced he encountered an angel. Well, at least we are certain that God put someone in his path to remind him where he would end up if he decided to let Satan win and have a drink. So by the time Kenny stepped through our doors, he was a little cooled off. He told me he had talked to the pastor of the church we had attended on and off over the years. Kenny informed me he would only speak to me if I agreed to meet with the pastor the next day. Of course, I would. I was not giving up on us and I let him know I would do whatever it would take to save our marriage.

Before the meeting with the pastor, Kenny recovered all the deleted texts from my phone. By the time he was at the church, he was enraged. When I arrived, he was screaming at the top of his lungs, showing the pastor the texts. As you can imagine, having the pastor and Kenny see those texts was embarrassing. I was not proud at all. It was not what I said but what I allowed the man to say. None of it was honoring to my marriage. Kenny was so angry, as he had a right to be. He sat across from me and would not look at me. The pastor started with a prayer followed by trying to get the details of what happened to bring us to this point. We each took turns and gave our side. He asked us if we believed we had a good marriage, besides the incident that got us in his office. We both answered yes. He asked us if we both wanted the marriage to work out. I said yes, and Kenny said he was not sure.

Because of Kenny's anger, the pastor thought it would be safer for everyone if I found somewhere else to stay for a while. He called it a biblical separation. I had no idea where I was supposed to go. My only option was to call our middle daughter and see if I could crash with her. She was willing to put me up but was unsure how long I could stay. I made arrangements for James to stay with his dad. Kenny still had my phone and continued combing through it, looking for proof of other inappropriate relationships or friendships. He looked through all of my social media, emails, texts, and any place he thought he might find evidence that I was lying.

The first night away was awful. I do not think I slept more than a few hours. I could not eat; nothing tasted good, and my stomach was in the tightest knots it had ever been in. I had no way to communicate with anyone, and I was not sure I would ever see my phone, house, belongings, or husband again. Although I felt ashamed for what I did to cause this, I was also mad at Kenny. I knew he had been masturbating and using porn on and off for so many years now. How were my actions any worse than his? I believed what he was doing was cheating too, so didn't he have a part to play in this mess? Wasn't he to be held accountable for his dysfunction?

Reflection Questions For Section 4

1. Consider the story of Hosea and Gomer (Hosea 1-3), which illustrates God's enduring love and faithfulness despite human unfaithfulness. How does this story offer you hope in the midst of relational dysfunction? How can seeking God's wisdom help recognize and navigate dysfunctional patterns in relationships?

2. Reflect on the decision to enter into a new relationship or marriage after experiencing dysfunction. What factors influenced your choice? Did you ignore familiar or similar dysfunction in your new relationship? Describe a moment when you realized history was repeating itself. How did you respond?

3. If you struggle with any form of addiction, how can surrendering the bondage of addiction to God lead to freedom and healing? How does reliance on God's grace enable you to break free from the chains of addiction? What steps can you take to surrender the cycle of addiction and its effects on your relationships to God?

4. Read Matthew 6:19-21 "Don't store up for yourselves treasures on earth, where moth and rust destroy and where thieves break in and

steal. But store up for yourselves treasure in heaven, where neither moth nor rust destroys, and where thieves don't break in and steal. For where your treasure is, there your heart will be also." Where have you spent time and energy storing up your treasures? If they were earthly things, have they been destroyed or stolen? What is your heart set on? What would you have to reprioritize or change in order to set your heart on heavenly things?

5. What role does prayer play in your life? In your relationship with God? Do you believe in the power of prayer? Why do you think God wants us to spend time with Him in prayer? How could you make time in your daily life to prioritize prayer?

SECTION 5

FINDING REAL FREEDOM

"How joyful is the one whose transgression is forgiven, whose sin is covered! How joyful is a person whom the Lord does not charge with iniquity and in whose spirit is not deceit!"

Psalms 32-1-2 (CSB)

CHAPTER 27

Let The Healing Begin

S omehow, I knew I needed to run to God. I knew I needed Him more now than I ever did. I opened my Bible and found myself right where God wanted me: the Psalms. As I read, God's Word was like a comfortable blanket I wrapped around myself after coming in from a bone-chilling winter day. I curled up in the Lord's lap and let His words hold me tight. I sobbed and cried out to Him to take away my pain, fear, and anxiety. I asked Him to do what I knew only He could: heal and help me. Rescue me from myself.

I was finally able to admit I was trying to play God in my own life and trying to be in control of everything because I was a mess. I realized instead of God being number one, I was putting everything above Him. My idols included shopping, clothes, my looks, attention from others, people's perception of me, trying to feel good/pretty enough, food, reality TV shows, my pride, ego, self-worth, lying, flirting, and trying to control Kenny.

After a few days there was a miracle. Kenny prayed and asked God to help him with our situation. My husband was asking for clarity—what he should do, what he should believe, and if he could trust or forgive me. Kenny heard God tell him if you want to know the truth, you have to tell the truth. So the following day, Kenny called the pastor and told him he was ready to meet and talk. Kenny contacted our daughter and arranged for her to bring me to the church at the time of the meeting. When I saw Kenny, my heart melted from guilt and pain. I wanted to run over to him, kiss and hold him, and tell him everything would be okay. Kenny was quiet as we entered the pastor's office. I sat on the couch, and Kenny sat across from me on a chair. After prayer, the pastor asked us each again if we were ready to see what God could do for our marriage. I replied I was willing to do anything. He then turned and asked Kenny. He said he needed me to answer some questions, and my answers would determine how we moved forward. The pastor told us that to heal our marriage, we both had to be completely honest and put it all on the table.

The pastor had us each write down what we wanted to confess. I wrote down everything I had lied to Kenny about regarding the trip to Vegas and the relationship with the man from the engineering company. I shared with Kenny and the pastor all the ways I was not truthful to the best of my memory. For now, he was satisfied with the things I was revealing and being honest about. When it was Kenny's turn, he shared the truth about his porn use over the years. My intuition was validated. I share with the pastor and Kenny that I had known it happened repeatedly for years. The pastor pointed out that both of us were outside the bonds of marriage, and we both had broken our covenant vows. We both had committed a form of adultery against the other. We had shared something meant only for our spouse with someone or something else or ourselves. We both had sinned against God and our marriage.

Our pastor then informed us there were some steps we had to take. First, he asked both of us if we were willing to submit and surrender all of ourselves over to God and let Him be the leader in our lives. I turned to Kenny and said I hoped he would make the same choice as me. I confessed right there I was sick and tired of being sick and tired, and I wanted to be free from all my pain. I told Kenny I was all in for Jesus, and from that day forward, God would be my number one guy. I was choosing to put God before Kenny, my children, grandchildren, our dog, our friends, our families, our possessions, our work, food, shopping, my ego, my insecurities, my hurts, my childhood wounds, being rejected by my father and all the others in my life, my desires, my hopes, and my dreams. All of it! Thankfully, Kenny made the same choice. We prayed and recommitted our lives to Christ and each other.

Next, our pastor asked each of us if we were willing to do whatever the other person needed the other to do to rebuild trust. We both said yes. I agreed to change my cell phone number, remove men's numbers from my contact list, and delete all existing texts to start fresh. Kenny was allowed to check my phone any time he asked to, and he wanted me to delete pictures from my phone that triggered him, like from the trip to Vegas. We both agreed to get off social media, and if a guy wanted my number, I was to give them Kenny's number. He needed me to stop watching reality TV (and delete all saved episodes from our DVR). I was to show Kenny all my receipts for accountability on my spending. There would be no drinking in public, no concerts without Kenny, and no single friends' outings. We agreed on things Kenny needed to do on his own and things we wanted to do as a couple. We would do both individual and couples counseling, attend Celebrate Recovery, pray together at least two times a day, read the Bible daily, and have our own private times with God.

We started going to the marriage class at the church we had been attending. They had just finished a study and were a few weeks from beginning the new curriculum. During the transition to the new study, the leaders showed a few videos and taught about them. One of the speakers we watched was Jimmy Evans. Kenny and I both liked what we heard him say. He seemed so wise, honest, and relatable. Later that week, I researched Jimmy Evans and learned he had a TV show, a podcast, and some books I could read.

I ordered *Marriage On The Rock* and *The Four Laws of Love* immediately. I searched on TV for anything Jimmy Evans was involved with and found the *Marriage Today* program. I recorded all the episodes I could. Kenny and I would sit and watch as many as our hearts and minds could handle. We were soaking it all up like sponges. Everything Jimmy Evans said made sense, and he pointed to many areas where we had allowed Satan into our own lives and our marriage. Jimmy reinforced what we agreed to in the pastor's office: to put God first in our lives and at the center of our marriage.

Things were not always easy during the early days of our healing journey. There were good days and bad days, easier days and challenging days. Kenny and I were doing whatever we could to learn how God wanted us to live for Him, His kingdom, and our marriage. Over those roller-coaster days and nights, I learned to rely on God, lean into Him, feel His presence, trust in His timing, and pray as I had never known I could. Besides listening, watching, and reading all things Jimmy Evans, we also found other pastors who resonated with us and whom we believe God brought to us to help us grow spiritually and relationally: Steven Furtick, Tony Evans, and believe it or not, Phil Robertson of Duck Dynasty. I read every marriage book I could get my hands on: *The Meaning of Marriage* by Timothy Keller, *Sacred Marriage* by Gary Thomas, *Love & Respect* by Dr. Emerson Eggerichs, and *The 5 Love Languages* by Gary Chapman, just to name a few. Two books that were instrumental in healing the wounds caused to both of us by porn were *Every Man's Battle* and *Every Heart Restored* by Stephen Auterburn.

Finally, the marriage class was ready to start the new study. It was *How We Love* by Milan and Kay Yerkovich. We would learn how our upbringing, especially in the first few years of life, influenced our marriage. We had to take a test to determine which love style we had. I tested as a pleaser and Kenny as a controller. According to the authors, I had an anxious love style, and Kenny had a disorganized attachment wound. For the first time in our lives, we had an explanation for why we had made some of our life choices and why we had some of the fears we had about relationships. We felt heard, seen, and validated for the first time.

As things were heating up and getting to the juicy stuff in the class and book, COVID-19 shut it all down. Where we lived in California, the government was super strict about meeting people in person, so the church stopped all classes and services. We were about to start exploring how to dig deeper and expose the roots of our wounded love styles when it felt like the rug was pulled out from under our chairs. The wounds were exposed, and it felt like we were bleeding from the jugular with no way to bandage ourselves up. I wouldn't let this stop us, though, so I got to work. I found videos online to accompany the book and workbook. Kenny and I waded through the questions, opened up our hearts, and allowed the Holy Spirit to do the work in us.

As the world closed itself off and shut us in our house, we took the time to heal and grow. God was moving mountains. He was replacing lies in our hearts and minds with His truth. God showed us what had happened in our early lives that left us injured and exposed. He taught us how to identify these damaged areas. He showed us how to feel feelings we had pushed down and ignored for years. We trusted Him with those raw, vulnerable parts of our hearts and souls for the first time in either of our lives. According to Kay and Milan Yerkovich neither of us had learned how to feel and deal with our families of origin. We were looking at our past not to blame but rather to explain how and why we made the choices we did in our lives. We studied how our childhood experiences shaped us and created patterns of how we accepted and received love that we brought into the marriage with us.

The process went quicker for me than for Kenny. God was able to use me to help facilitate Kenny's healing and bring him to a place of trust he had never experienced in his life. Each of us was now able to give our hurts to God. He showed both of us how we were harming ourselves as well as our marriage. We learned new ways of dealing with the things that got in our way as a couple. We knew what types of things triggered each of us. We learned how to communicate in a way that was good for our injuries and each other's. We had empathy and sympathy for each other in ways we could not before. We understood where the scars and dysfunction came from, so we learned not to take what was going on in the other person personally. We were able to express our needs and desires to each other, and we were able to fulfill the needs of the other person in a way that was right for them. We learned how to do life and marriage God's way.

During all of this, we discovered Kenny needed neck surgery. In July 2020 he ended up having three vertebrae in his neck fused. This actually worked out really well because it gave us more time to spend in God's Word, do Bible studies, watch Jimmy Evans, listen to podcasts, and read marriage books. After healing our souls, hearts, minds, and bodies, God put it on our hearts to work with other struggling couples. What He had done for us—how He had healed us—God was directing us to go out and show others. We started working one-on-one with couples that God sent our direction. He had also placed a couple in our lives that would become our marriage coaching mentors. They had been involved in marriage ministry longer than Kenny and I had been married. They showed us the ropes, answered all our questions, and prepared us to be available when and where God called us while teaching us how to set up boundaries and protection for our marriage.

CHAPTER 28

Following God To Texas

At the end of September, Kenny's doctor released him to start working again. He was a little slower, but the average person would not have noticed. Kenny would work hard during the day. In the evenings and on weekends we would go to church events, lead as small group leaders at Celebrate Recovery, attended our Monday night Bible study, and helped mentor struggling couples. It wasn't long before all of this was weighing on Kenny physically. COVID was also making things hard for a small business owner. Materials were tough to acquire, and employees were either getting sick and having to stay home or deciding it was easier to collect unemployment than show up for work. Kenny cried out to God, "How much longer will I have to work like this to pay the bills? How much longer will my body hurt? Please show me Your plan for my life." God was about to show us an answer to Kenny's cries but not in a way we expected at all.

Our oldest son, Luke, decided to move from California to Dallas, Texas. He needed help moving his roommate's car along with all their other possessions. I suggested I drive one car to Texas for them as long as they paid for my flight home. Kenny was working on an extensive remodel project with many phases, so he would stay and work while I went with Luke and his friend. But COVID struck again. Kenny could not complete a section of his stonework on the front of this house because the windows had not arrived. They were delayed for about two or three weeks, so this freed him up to accompany me on the road trip to Texas. We decided to make the trip to Texas a vacation, see some family on the way, and visit a few hot rod shops from the TV shows Kenny likes to watch.

In early March, we loaded our luggage in our son's roommate's car and set out on an adventure. Our first stop was Vegas to see our daughter Valarie, the grandchildren, and a few of those hot rod shops. Next, we headed out toward Dallas. We made it to Amarillo and stayed for the evening. Our son called and said they got a late start, so they were delayed. This gave us a day to kill, so I suggested to Kenny that since we were close to Oklahoma, we stop and see another hot rod shop from another show he watched. So we headed out for OKC.

From there, we headed toward Dallas with a detour to see Kenny's cousin, who had moved to East Texas in December 2020. As we dropped into Texas from Oklahoma, I was convinced we were not in Texas. It was so green, and there were trees everywhere—real trees! I assumed all of Texas was dry, dusty, and hot like West Texas. When Luke was in the Navy, we had traveled to see him graduate from A school in San Antonio. During that trip, Kenny and I both said out loud we would never move to Texas since there was not a tree in sight and it was so flat. But East Texas was beautiful. Everything was so green, and the pine trees reminded me of being close to where we lived in CA.

Once we got to our cousin's house, said our hellos, and got the tour of their place, they informed us the property next to theirs was for sale. We thought, *Okay, that's great, but what does that have to do with us?* They told us we should sell our home in California and move to East Texas next to them. The price of the land was unheard of compared to California prices, but how could we know if we would even like the area? What would we be able to sell our house for, and what on earth would it cost to build a house from the ground up in East Texas? These were all things I would need to think about before even considering a move. So first things first: where are the closest gas stations, grocery stores, Target, and Ulta? And what about churches?

The cousins drove us around for the day, showing us the sights and pointing out all that is good and great about East Texas. We talked about the cost of living, working conditions, housing prices, politics, taxes, churches, and shopping, among a few things. It all looked and sounded convincing, but maybe this part of Texas was a mirage, and the rest was not to our liking and looked more like West Texas. Kenny and I decided if this decision was really on the table, we needed to investigate further. So on our way to meet our son, we drove all over. We went through every small town we could in the two weeks we were there. North to the border, as far East as we could and still be in the state, South a few hours, back West towards Waco, and from there up to Dallas and beyond. During this driving, we talked, explored, contemplated, and dreamed, but most importantly, we prayed about whether the Holy Spirit was leading us to do this.

We also needed this to make financial sense. I made some calculations and let Kenny know that for us to leave California, our children, our business, and the house we poured our heart and soul into, it had to be a specific amount. He assured me he was on the same page. As we visited with our son, we saw as many Texas sights as we could that week. We were praying and dreaming about if God was planning a move for us here. After our three weeks of travel and fun, we flew home.

We both agreed the first step was to have a relator over. The relator spent about two hours with us reviewing the house—the good things and the things that may need to be fixed before we put it on the market. After the tour, she sat down at our table, made some calculations, and wrote down the price she believed she could list the house for. When she handed the paper to us, it was the exact number God had given us. We were shocked! Kenny and I knew this could mean only one thing: God wanted us to list the house, sell it, and move to East Texas.

Right there, we signed on the dotted line and listed the house for sale. The relator left us with a list of to-dos that needed to be completed before we put the house on the market. It was the last week in March. Before we got to work, we had to have a difficult conversation with our youngest son, James. We asked him about his intentions for moving forward in masonry and taking over the business. He said he was unsure whether it was his passion or a job. Then we asked him if he wanted to move to Texas with us. James answered with a very quick and resounding NO! He would not leave all of his best friends and the town he loved. It saddened me that he did not want to move with us, but Kenny and I knew without a shadow of a doubt that God was orchestrating this and opening our doors to move.

We got busy preparing the house for pictures, listing, and showings. Three weeks later, the house was listed. After a few short days, we accepted an offer *above* the asking price. What on earth? God was moving, and He was moving fast. We had a closing date for the last week in May and had an exact amount we would walk with, so we felt comfortable moving ahead with the relator in East Texas. She went right to work for us. We flew out four or five times, looking at perspective houses. Nothing. God had not found us our new house yet. We still trusted Him, knowing He wanted us somewhere in East Texas.

It was almost time to leave our California house, and there was still no Texas home. Being obedient is scary—sometimes terrifying—but we followed wherever God led us. The third week in May, we moved all our belongings to a storage facility in East Texas, minus our mattress, a few clothes, and the work tools Kenny would need. During the last week in California, we began to think we had not heard God correctly—not about the move but rather about what region He wanted us in. We began to devise a plan to travel outside of Texas into Tennessee and North Carolina. We continued praying that God would show us where He wanted us. Was it easy? No. Was it scary? Yes. But we both had a peace we knew with all our hearts that could only come from God.

During the last few days in our house in California, I was looking online at houses for sale in East Texas. I scrolled past a house for sale by an owner in a little town that was on the top of our list. It was in our price range, was very clean, and had only been on the market for minutes. I called my realtor, and she scheduled an immediate appointment. She viewed the home, sent us pictures and videos, and told us that it fit most of what we sought. Kenny and I jumped. We put in an offer, prayed, and believed that no matter what happened, God had a plan. Forty-five minutes later, as we drove to our Monday night Bible study group, our relator called us with the news: they accepted our offer! Two days later, after we had said our final goodbyes to family and friends, we left California with our remaining belongings and headed for our new house, in a new state, for a new season of life in East Texas.

CHAPTER 29

Searching For A New Church

O ne of the first things Kenny and I wanted to do was find a church. Before we left California, I did what I do best: I researched. I googled local churches, viewed their websites, looked at their belief statements online, checked them out on Facebook, and watched videos on YouTube. I had a list of over fourteen churches we wanted to check out as we settled. Again, we prayed and asked God to put us where He wanted us. During the first week, as we were busy getting utilities turned on, we stopped at the electric company in person. We had to be escorted back to a manager's office to fill out papers and leave a deposit. In this woman's office were pictures of her family and wooden signs inscribed with Scriptures, which let us know she was a Christian. I asked her where she attended church. When she gave me the name, I scanned my list. There it was! The manager did a very bold thing and invited us to service on Sunday. Kenny and I decided to start with her church since we had an invite and would recognize at least one person.

That very Sunday, we walked through the doors. Some friendly people standing at the entrance greeted us right off the bat. They recognized we were new and ushered us over to the welcome table. In exchange for filling out our information, we each got a free church T-shirt. Kenny and I took a bulletin and sat about three rows from the front. We ended up sitting in the same row as the woman who invited us. She was so excited to see us there and introduced us to a few others sitting around where we were. She apologized as she told us the pastor was out of town and they had a guest speaker. Service started with worship. The music was beautifully done and modern, and it sounded amazing. The speaker was a young woman who was a church member but was currently living and working in Hatti. She shared her testimony about how God had moved her, quickly taking care of all the arrangements. As she was speaking, Kenny and I turned to each other. This was how God had worked in our lives to get us to East Texas.

The service was powerful for both Kenny and me. He was ready to decide to become a member right then and there. He said he felt the Holy Spirit telling him this was where we needed to be. I was not ready to make such a quick decision. After all, I had thirteen more churches on my list to check out. I suggested we choose a different church for the next four Sundays and then see. Kenny wanted to return the following Sunday, and he asked how we could decide based on moving around each Sunday. He wanted to spend some time at each one. I was okay with maybe doing four Sundays at each church until we found the right fit. Well, guess what? After just a few Sundays and asking God for direction, Kenny and I felt welcomed and believed this was the church God had called us to.

CHAPTER 30

Gearing Up For Ministry

Kenny had to travel back to California to finish some work, so we could attend church together for only two or three weeks. At first, I told him I would be willing to visit a few of the other churches on my list while he was away. But that never happened. I felt comfortable and very welcomed at the original one we visited. Kenny and I started to ask God in our prayer time how He wanted to use us at this church. We prayed with open hearts and minds and quietly listened for confirmation and direction from the Holy Spirit, God's Word, or someone in the church to say something God sent them to say. While Kenny was away, I met with the pastor to tell him more about us, understand the church better, see if gaps needed to be filled, and ask where Kenny and I could plug in. As we talked, the pastor mentioned they did not have anyone teaching a marriage class, and they didn't have a marriage ministry. My ears perked up, and my heart danced because this is where we believed God was leading us, but we did not want to presume anything. We wanted to let God tell us where He needed us in this church, and He did!

I called Kenny and told him. We were sure this is why God brought us to this little town in East Texas and this particular church. We continued to pray for direction in what that would look like. In the meantime, we couldn't start until Kenny was back from California, so I studied up on all my marriage materials, especially *Marriage on The Rock* and *The Four Laws of Love*, both books by Jimmy Evans. Kenny and I believed *Marriage on the Rock* was an excellent curriculum to start with; I think of it as an all-inclusive resort for marriage help. From cover to cover, Jimmy Evans packs it all in there: how to do marriage God's way, because when you do, you have a 100 percent chance of success.

As I dove into *The Four Laws of Love* while preparing for teaching, God brought to my attention an area of my life and my marriage that was still not free from sin. It was the fourth law Jimmy talked about, which is called the law of purity. Genesis 2:25 says, "Both the man and his wife were naked, yet felt no shame." (CSB). I had lied to people about what I had done or not done all those years. I had kept all the cover-up from Kenny about stupid stuff and not-so-stupid stuff. At the beginning of our relationship, I told him lies to protect myself and make myself seem more attractive so he would like me. I had kept telling these lies over the years because I believed what I started I could never stop, even now after all we had been through and all God had healed us from. God was using this book and this time away from Kenny to peel back another layer of my dysfunction and sin.

I felt led to come clean to Kenny about everything I had lied to him about over the years. The Holy Spirit was nudging me to do it right then and there, over the phone. I was so scared, but I knew I had to obey God. I knew this was the time He had ordained for this revealing. I was shaking as I dialed Kenny's number. I started by telling him I loved him and had to be in a place where all my sin was confessed, so I was ready to teach others how to do the same. I could not expect our students to learn and implement what I had yet to do myself. So I took a deep breath and knew that no matter what happened next, God would never leave or forsake me. He was my firm foundation, and I could trust that He would provide for me if I obeyed what He asked me to do.

I confessed right then all of the things that I could remember I had lied to him about. Kenny was not shocked and he said, "I already knew that, and I was wondering when you would tell me." I am amazed at how he still loved me and how patient he was with me, and I understand why he had difficulty trusting me all these years. Before we hung up the phone, we prayed. Kenny assured me despite how hard some of what I revealed to him was to hear, he could deal with the truth.

At the end of August 2021, we decided to go away to Galveston and spend a few days at the beach having a vision retreat. We learned about doing a vision retreat from Jimmy Evans a few years back in California. It is one of the ways you help keep your marriage fresh. The goal is to set aside a few days where you and your spouse can pray, talk about, and negotiate for all areas of your relationship—money, children, vacations, sex, communication, hopes, and dreams. There is a workbook that helps direct your steps. It helps alleviate unmet expectations and arguments. We spent a few hours in the morning talking about a specific topic. Each of us shared our desires for the year, and then we prayed about it. If we agreed, then we wrote it down. We also took breaks and played and had fun. After a few hours, we returned to the room and repeated the process with another subject off our list. If we disagreed on something, we did not move on until God has clarified it for us. Because God sees us as one, if we disagree, we believe that in itself is an answer—it is a "no" or "not right now."

Since we moved and so many things had changed, we thought we had better get away and ask God for direction. What were His plans for us in East Texas? What did He want us to do for the marriage ministry at the church? What did He want us to do for income? Was Kenny supposed to do masonry and concrete? What about me? Was I supposed to get a job outside the home, outside our usual business? While praying and talking, God sent me to the XO Marriage website. I was looking to see if XO Marriage certified people in *Marriage on the Rock*. While on the website, I noticed that XO Marriage offered a certificate program for spouses to become certified marriage mediators. I read more about it, shared the info with Kenny, and asked him what he thought. He said, "Let's bring it to God." So we did.

In our quiet time, God told us to contact XO Marriage for more information about the mediator training. I left an email for the mediator coordinator. After a few days, we had clarity about most of the areas on our vision retreat list. God was transparent about the direction He wanted us to go with the class at the church.

Not long after our Vison Retreat, Kenny was back in California finishing up more work. While he was gone, I set up the classroom at the church. I decorated the room with Scriptures and quotes from marriage gurus, like Jimmy Evans, Tim Keller, Gary Thomas, and Milan and Kay Yerkovich. Each table had our class rules in the center, placed in a small table tent. There were pens and pencils, note cards for prayer requests, a box of tissues, and a decorative touch. We wanted the room to feel as cozy as possible and to be inviting for the couples to share openly. We wanted them to feel like they were sitting with us in our living room, not in a large, cold space.

CHAPTER 31

Amazing Training

While Kenny was home for a short stay before he had to fly back to California, I received an email reply from XO Marriage. I opened it up as fast as I could! The email gave me specifics about the marriage meditation certification, and I learned there were only two spots left in the next class. I knew this was God. I rushed out to the shop where Kenny was preparing for his trip back, and through tears, I told him what was in the email and asked his thoughts. He, too, believed God held these last two spots for us. He instructed me to run back into the house and register before someone else got them.

Over the next few weeks, from California and East Texas, we prepared for the class. We received a list of prerequisites to be completed before the in-person teaching. I spent as much time as I could watching the videos, reading the materials, and doing all the things and then some to prepare. Kenny and I talked daily while apart about the curriculum and what we were learning. God is so cool. Even when you think you have it all figured out and are doing pretty well, He shows you more ways and places you need healing in, areas where you are falling short. Kenny and I grew even more during this time in our understanding of who God is and how much He loves us.

The day of the twenty-hour in-person training could not come fast enough for me. I was excited to learn, meet new people, and be at XO Marriage in person. I was not sure what to expect, but I think deep down, I was hoping to see or meet Pastor Jimmy. He played such a large part in our marriage transformation. I wanted to shake his hand and tell him "Thank you" in person.

I remember walking into the XO Marriage offices and conference room. I had the weirdest feeling inside, like I was coming home. When I swung open the doors and walked up the stairs to the conference room, I had a calm, warm, "just walked into my childhood home after being away at college for the semester" kind of feeling. At that moment, I told Kenny we were supposed to be here. I said I had no idea what was happening inside of me, but this was something special we were doing. I could only imagine what God was and would be doing in us and through us.

I learned so many amazing things those two days. It was so powerful to be in a room with other people whose hearts desire to see marriages survive and thrive. The staff was so welcoming and made us feel right at home, and we wanted for nothing over the two full days. We met some XO Marriage celebrities like Dave and Ashley Willis and Tim Ross. Teresa and Pam lead the class with passion and insight, and they are full of the Holy Spirit. On day two, something profound happened to me. Allen Kelsey, who co-wrote a book with Jimmy Evans called *Strengths-Based Marriage*, was the morning's first speaker. Each trainee was to take the StrengthFinder test. In this test, you answer questions, and your answers are formulated into a particular order of the talents and traits God hardwired you for. There are thirty-four of these traits, and each human has a specific order, with only a few people on earth with the same top five as you.

At the beginning of his lesson, Allan asked for one man and one woman in the class to reveal their top five. I was sitting right in front of him, so I spoke up: learner, focus, discipline, input, and achiever. He started by explaining how mediators can use these strength results to help couples learn more about their spouses. He said it is a valuable tool in understanding why your spouse does some of the things they do—not to irritate you but because God has created them in this unique, particular way. Then, Allan explained how different strengths would present in a marriage relationship, how a person may or may not like to handle situations, and how they would approach life.

Next, he came to my top five. As I listened to him explain who I was based on these traits, the room grew silent. I was only focused on Allan's words. I started to feel as if I was the only one in the room who he was talking to. My heart began to beat faster, my hands shook, and I could not hold back tears. He was telling me exactly who I was. What I had been like all my life. What I would be good at and excel in. The best way to describe it is to say it was like someone had been following me all my life and taking notes. I felt seen—really seen—for the first time in my life. I was visibly shaken, and Kenny reached over and put his hand on mine.

During the break, Kenny asked me what had happened. Even Pam came up to me and asked if I was okay. I could not describe what I felt had happened right there, but something changed for me. I tried to explain it to Kenny and the others who asked, but my words were inadequate. It wasn't until Kenny and I were on our way home that it hit me. The only way I can describe it was as if Allan's voice was really God's voice, telling me how he created me, and who He created me to be. I felt truly accepted, loved, cherished, wanted and needed deep in my soul. I cried again as I shared my realization with Kenny.

Before we left to head home, a few members of the XO team invited us to attend the last XO conference of the year. Kenny and I signed up and booked a room on the way home. We would head back to Dallas in a few weeks and attend our first XO Conference in person. Just like the training, XO puts on a first-class event. We walked around, bought swag like books and t-shirts, and did a meet and greet with Dave and Ashley Willis as well as Scott and Vanessa Martindale from Blended Kingdom Families.

At this conference, one of the speakers was Julia Jeffress Sadler. She spoke on the importance of dreaming and praying big for your marriage. I bought her book, read it cover to cover, and told Kenny, "Let's make our list of big things we want to do this next year." Some of the items included being able to train table leaders for the marriage class at church, hold a dance and marriage gathering at the church, learn to better communicate how our marriage is part of God's story, remodel the house, pray for a few family members who are not saved yet, meet members of Kenny's family in person whom he had never met before, memorize more Scriptures, sell our Harley motorcycle, and a few other "little" things. But the number one on our list—the big one for us—was to work with XO Marriage.

For the rest of that year Kenny and I taught the marriage class at the church. We set it up to watch videos, teach lessons, and have discussions and fellowship. During this time, we met with couples who needed one-on-one help. We had couples we met with a few times a month, some once a week, and others who participated in our one and two day intensives.

CHAPTER 32

Big Things

I n January 2022, Kenny and I decided God was leading us to turn the marriage ministry into a coaching business. God would use this time during our morning walks for inspiration and revelation, and He gave Kenny the name for the business: Marriage In Motion:365. We prayed about it and believed in it. This name tells us that marriage must always be moving forward—in motion—healing, learning, and growing, and there is never a day off. It is a three hundred and sixty-five-day commitment to God, your spouse, and yourself.

As spring blossomed, God started placing in us restlessness about the church we were at. We continued to teach the class and minister to and mentor couples in need, but something was calling us somewhere else. Kenny and I prayed to make sure it was not us making this decision, but instead, we were in God's will for us, our business, the couples we were working with, and the church.

One particular church always caught our eye, mainly because it reminded us of our church in California. Something or someone always made us turn and look as we drove by. So we decided to go there on Mother's Day Sunday. We also chose this church because it was about the same distance from our house as the church we were currently attending (just in the opposite direction). As we entered through the doors held open by volunteers, one of the first people we met was the marriage and family pastor. That was no accident. We explained a little about who we were and that God prompted us to be there that day. The worship music was uplifting, and the message spoke to Kenny and me in a way only God could orchestrate.

Each time we visited the message always hit right to the core of our prayers about being there. We attended the new member's class where we learned about their operations, beliefs, values, and mission. God kept speaking to us through the leaders and the other members. On several separate occasions, people we had never met spoke prophetic words into our lives, specifically over me and writing this book.

Kenny and I were planning to travel from the end of July until late August. We wanted to have a clear answer from God about the decision to leave our current church and see if this new one was where He was calling us. We agreed to fast and be in serious prayer. On July 1, we started the fast, and on Sunday, July 3, we believe God used Jason John Cowart to answer some of our prayers. After worship, Jason walked on stage and introduced himself to those of us who were new and did not know him. One of the first things he talked about was how this church raised him spiritually and sent him on his way to open and lead his church. Jason said if anyone was there and was looking for a church where they could be fed, challenged, and grow in their relationship with God, it was here at this church. As he finished saying this, Kenny and I turned in unison and looked at each other with wide eyes. We were both thinking, *Was this confirmation?* Then Jason held up his latest book and talked about it. He said copies would be sold in the lobby after service if anyone were interested. Then he stopped, looked out at the congregation, and pointing his finger, tracing the crowd, he said, "I am not sure, but God is telling me someone here today needs to write their book. They need to tell their story, and God is telling you to do it now." Again, Kenny and I nearly broke our necks, turning to look at each other so fast. Was this message again for me? This was the third person in two weeks who spoke to me about writing.

We wanted to make sure Kenny and I were following God's will for our lives, so we did not make a final decision that day. But those things became part of our prayers to God. We kept praying and fasting all of July. By the end of the month, Kenny and I believed we had a clear answer from God. Kenny called our current pastor and told him God was calling us away from this church. It was a hard call, but when you follow God and live in His will, there is so much peace, even in the most complex decisions you will ever have to make. Besides, Kenny and I had spent most of our lives living in disobedience to God, and we knew how destructive and painful that can be. We now move whenever and wherever God calls us.

Kenny and I called the couples who were part of our class to tell them personally about our decision. They were shocked but understood. We reassured them we were leaving the church but not them. They could call, text, or email whenever needed. We explained our mentoring services would always be available to them, and we wanted to stay in touch and make sure we created time to see them in person, not just as teachers and mentors but also as friends and support.

We traveled in July and August as we had planned. When we returned home, we spent the next few months doing everything a person needs to do to grow a business. We created a website, got our emails set up, made business cards, started social media accounts for Marriage In Motion:365, set goals for growth, and developed procedures and curriculum. We also had to ensure we were growing in our personal lives and learning all we could about becoming marriage coaches. We took courses on line and in person, attended seminars from our speakers and writers, listened to lots of podcasts, read every book we could get our hands on and continued focusing on attachment theory and wounds.

While we were busy doing this, we continued attending XO Marriage events and supporting the ministry we loved and held dear to our hearts. It always inspired us to attend their conferences, date night events, or book launches. We even got to tour and sign drywall at the new building XO was constructing in Southlake, Texas. Kenny and I kept praying from our list of big things for the year, trusting in God and His plans for us, Marriage In Motion:365, those people on our list, and especially my hopes and desires as they pertained to XO Marriage.

In the last month of 2022, God answered one of those prayers in a big way. We received a call from XO Marriage asking if Kenny and I wanted to become part of the in-house mediation team. They wanted us to pray over the offer and seek God's will in this for us, and they would reach out to us in a couple of weeks. Those days felt like an eternity for me, waiting for the call back to tell them we would be honored to be part of the team. It was official; Kenny and I became in-house XO Marriage Mediators at the beginning of 2023.

Reflection Questions For Section 5

1. Define freedom in your own words. What does true freedom mean to you? Look like to you? Reflect on a time when you felt truly free. What circumstances contributed to that feeling? Reflect on John 8:36 "So if the Son sets you free, you will be free indeed." How does this verse capture the ultimate source of real freedom?

2. What does having a real relationship with Christ look like to you? How can you cultivate a deeper, intimate relationship in your own life with Christ?

3. What do you believe your life would look like or be like if you fully surrendered all of yourself and your ways to following Gods design for life and relationships? How does surrendering to God's way lead to freedom from the chains of sin and dysfunction? How does surrendering to God's ways bring about freedom from fear, anxiety and insecurity?

4. Read 2 Corinthians 5:17 "Therefore, if anyone is in Christ, he is a new creation; the old has passed away, and see the new has come!" What are the old things you have to get rid of to be a new creation?

5. Reflect on Proverbs 3:5-6 "Trust in the Lord with all your heart, and do not rely on your own understanding; in all your ways know him, and he will make your path straight. In your life, how have you relied on your own understanding? What would it look like in your life to trust God with all of your heart?

Conclusion

THE NEXT 50 YEARS

I don't know if it is part of God's plan to have me on Earth for another fifty years. With the longevity on my mother's side, it very well could be. What I do know is, I will strive to do my best and put God first in all areas of my life. I spent too many years searching for acceptance and my identity in all the wrong places. All along it has been with me from the moment I said "I Do" to Christ at 9 years old.

I don't like to look back on my life and blame or feel shame. I want to understand what I went through and why I made the choices I did so I can learn and grow. I desire to share how God opened my eyes to His truth. I want to be able to tell others how, who, where, and when. My story and testimony are God's story and God's glory. My goal is to keep moving forward to the prize that I know is ahead.

I want this book to be a lamp on a stand to show that no matter how your life began, the choices you made, the ups, the downs, the mistakes, the heartache, the misery, the good, the great, all of it. He alone is where you will find freedom. He accepts you—all of you, warts and all. He doesn't even see the warts. He only sees the most beautiful thing He created long before the world was formed. And because of the blood of Jesus, He does not see the mess and madness that was done to us or that we did to ourselves. He removes all the shame and guilt. He sees us as white as snow.

If you do not know about the freedom I am talking about, please let me share with you where you can find it. Confess with your mouth that you believe Jesus came to Earth and lived a perfect, sinless life. He died on the cross for our sins, was placed in a tomb, and rose again on the third day. He is Lord! Allow God to come into your heart and ask Him to forgive you of all your sins.

Now you need to tell someone: a Christian friend, a pastor, a family member. Tell them about the best and most important decision you have ever made. As you can see from my story, it is not an easy road, but if, unlike me, you choose from this day forward to live first for God, He will make your paths straight (Proverbs 3:6). He will heal you of all the shame and guilt. He will heal you of all the painful experiences you had and all the wrong choices you made. He will heal your relationships, especially your marriage. He will give you a new life and a purpose. With God, all things are possible.

Bible Verses for Your Journey to Freedom

Scripture when you need comfort:

- Psalm 40:12-13 "For troubles without number have surrounded me: my inequities have overtaken me; I am unable to see. They are more than the hairs of my head, and my courage leaves me. Lord, be pleased to rescue me; hurry to help me, Lord."

- Philippians 4: 6-7 "Don't worry about anything, but in everything, through prayer and petition with thanksgiving, present your request to God. And the peace of God, which surpasses all understanding, will guard your hearts and minds in Christ Jesus."

- Isaiah 43:2-3a "When you pass though the waters, I will be with you, and the rivers will not overwhelm you. When you walk through the fire, you will not be scorched, and the flame will not burn you. For I am the Lord your God,"

- Isaiah 61:7 "In place of your shame you will have a double portion; in place of disgrace, they will rejoice over their share. So they will possess double in their land, and eternal joy will be theirs."

- Isaiah 40:31 "but those who trust in the Lord will renew their strength; they will soar on wings like eagles; they will run and not become weary, they will walk and not faint."

- Matthew 11:28 "Come to me, all of you who are weary and burdened, and I will give you rest."

- 2 Timothy 4:17-18 "But the Lord stood with me and strengthened me, so that I might fully preach the word and all the Gentiles might hear it. So I was rescued from the lion's mouth. The Lord will rescue me from every evil work and will bring me sagely into his heavenly kingdom. To him be the glory forever and ever! Amen."

- Micah 7:8 "Do not rejoice over me, my enemy! Though I have fallen, I will stand up; though I sit in darkness, the Lord will be my light."

- Psalm 106 (all of it)

- Psalm 118 (all of it)

Scripture to help you understand what is true about your sin:

- Matthew 6:21 "For where your treasure is, there your heart will be also."

- 1 John 1:9 "If we confess our sins, he is faithful and righteous to forgive us our sins and to cleanse us from all unrighteousness."

- James 4:1-3 "What is the source of wars and fights among you? Don't they come from your passions that wage war within you? You desire and you do not have. You murder and covet and cannot obtain. You fight and wage war. You do not have because you do not ask. You ask and don't receive because you ask with wrong motives, so that you may spend it on your pleasures."

- Romans 3:23 "For all have sinned and fall short of the glory of God;"

- Psalms 32:5 "Then I acknowledged my sin to you and did not conceal my iniquity. I said, "I will confess my transgressions to the lord," and you forgave the guilt of my sin."

- Psalms 32:1-2 "How joyful is the one whose transgression is forgiven, whose sin is covered! How joyful is a person whom the Lord does not charge with iniquity and in whose spirit is not deceit!"

- 1 Corinthians 6:11 "But you were washed, you were sanctified, you were justified in the name of the Lord Jesus Christ and by the Spirit of our God."

- Isaiah 1:18 "Come, let's settle this," says the Lord. "Though your sins are scarlet, they will be white as snow; though they are crimson red they will be like wool."

Scripture to know that your identity and acceptance come from God:

- Romans 8:38-39 "For I am persuaded that neither death nor life, nor angels nor rulers, nor things present nor things to come, nor powers, nor height nor depth, nor any other created thing will be able to separate us from the love of God that is in Christ Jesus our Lord."

- Ephesians 2:4-5 "But God, who is rich in mercy, because of his great love that he had for us, made us alive with Christ even though we were dead in trespasses. You are saved by grace.

- 1 Peter 2:9 "But you are a chosen race, a royal priesthood, a holy nation, a people for his possession, so that you may proclaim the praises of the one who called you out of the darkness into his marvelous light."

- Matthew 18:12-14 "What do you think? If someone has a hundred sheep, and one of them goes astray, won't he leave the ninety-nine on the hillside and go and search for the stray? And if he finds it, truly I tell you, he rejoices over that sheep more than over the ninety-nine that did not go astray. In the same way, it is not the will of your Father in heaven that one of these little ones perish."

- Psalm 139:13-14, 16 "For it was you who created my inward parts; you knit me together in my mother's womb. I will praise you because I have been remarkably and wondrously made. Your eyes saw me when I was formless; all my days were written in your book and planned before a single one of them began."

- Ephesians 2:10 "For we are his workmanship, created in Christ Jesus for good works, which God prepared ahead of time for us to do."

- Psalm 27:10 "Even if my father and mother abandon me, the Lord cares for me."

- John 6:37 "Everyone the Father gives me will come to me, and the one who comes to me I will never cast out."

- Isaiah 49:15 "Can a woman forget her nursing child, or lack compassion for the child of her womb? Even if these forget, yet I will not forget you."

- Deuteronomy 31:8 "The Lord is the one who will go before you. He will be with you; he will not leave you or abandon you. Do not be afraid or discouraged."

- 1 John 4:16 "And we come to know and to believe the love that God has for us. God is love, and the one who remains in love remains in God, and God remains in him."

Scripture about finding freedom in Christ:

- Philippians 2:13 "For it is God who is working in you both to will and to work according to his good purpose."

- Psalms 107: 13-14 "Then the cried out to the Lord in their trouble; he saved them from their distress. He brought them out of the darkness and gloom and broke their chains apart."

- Psalms 107: 19-20 "Then they cried out to the Lord in their trouble; he saved them from their distress. He sent his word and healed them; he rescued them from their traps."

- Romans 8: 1 "Therefore, there is now no condemnation for those in Christ Jesus, because the law of the Spirit of life in Christ Jesus has set you free from the law of sin and death."

- John 8:31b-32 "If you continue in my word, you really are my disciples. You will know the truth and the truth will set you free."

- John 4:14 "But whoever drinks from the water that I will give him will never get thirsty again. In fact, the water I will give him will become a well of water springing up in him for eternal life."

- Luke 8:47-48 "When the woman saw that she was discovered, she came trembling and fell down before him. In the presence of all the people, she declared the reason she had touched him and how she was instantly healed. "Daughter", he said to her, "your faith has saved you. Go in peace."

Scripture on how to have a relationship with Christ:

- Matthew 6:24 "No one can serve two masters, since either he will hate one and love the other, or he will be devoted to one and despise the other. You cannot serve both God and money."

- Matthew 6:33 "But seek first the kingdom of God and his righteousness, and all these things will be provided for you."

- Psalms 139: 23-24 "Search me, God, and know my heart; test me and know my concerns. See if there is any offensive way in me; lead me in the everlasting way."

- Proverbs 3: 5-6 "Trust in the Lord with all your heart, and do not rely on your own understanding; in all your ways know him, and he will make your path straight.

- James 4:8a "Draw near to God, and he will draw near to you."

- Proverbs 11:14 "Without guidance, a people will fall, but with many counselors there is deliverance."

- 1 Samuel 12:20-22 "Samuel replied, "Don't be afraid. Even though you have committed all this evil, don't turn away from following the Lord. Instead, worship the Lord with all your heart. Don't turn away to follow worthless things that can't profit or rescue you; they are worthless. The Lord will not abandon his people, because of his great name and because he has determined to make you his own people.""

- Colossians 3 (all of it)

- Romans 6 (all of it)

Further Reading & Resources

Marriage:

- Evans, Jimmy. (2012). *Marriage On The Rock.* XO Publishing.

- Evans, Jimmy. (2021). *The Four Laws of Love.* XO Publishing.

- Yerkovich, Kay and Milan. (2017). *How We Love. Expanded Edition. Discover Your Love Style, Enhance Your Marriage.* WaterBrook.

- Thomas, Gary. (2000). *Sacred Marriage.* Zondervan.

- Keller, Timothy. (2011). *The Meaning Of Marriage.* Penguin group.

- Cloud, Dr. Henry and Townsend, Dr. John. (1999). *Boundaries In Marriage.* Zondervan.

- Eggerichs, Dr. Emerson. (2004). *Love and Respect. The Love She Most Desires. The Respect He Desperately Needs.* W Publishing Group.

- Evans, Tony. (2016). *Kingdom Marriage. Connecting God's Purpose with Your Pleasure.* Tyndale House Publishing.

- Chapman, Gary. (2010). *The 5 Love Languages. The Secret to Love That Lasts.* Northfield Publishing.

- Parrott, Dr. Les and Leslie. (2001). *Saving Your Second Marriage Before It Starts. Nine Questions to Ask Before-and After-You Remarry.* Zondervan.

Blended Family:

- Martindale, Scott and Vanessa. (2022). *Blended & redeemed.* XO publishing.

- Becnel, Moe and Paige. *God Breathers on Blended Families.* (2009). Blending a Family Ministry.

Anger:

- Chapman, Gary. (2007). *Anger. Taming A Powerful Emotion.* Moody Publishers.

Porn:

- Evans, Jimmy. (2000). *A Mind Set Free. Overcoming Mental Strongholds Through Biblical Meditation.* XO Publishing.

- Arterburn, Stephen and Stoeker, Fred with Yorkey, Mike. (2000). *Every Man's Battle. Winning the War on Sexual Temptation. One Victory at a Time.* WaterBrook.

- Arterburn, Stephen and Stoeker, Fred and Brenda with Yorkey,

Mike. (2004). *Every Heart Restored. A Wife's Guide to Healing in the Wake of a Husband's Sexual Sin.* WaterBrook.

Food Struggles:

- Terkeurst, Lysa. (2010). *Made To Crave. Satisfying Your Deepest Desire with God, Not Food.* Zondervan.

- Cloninger, Claire and Barr, Laura. (1991). *Faithfully Fit. A 40-Day Devotional Plan to End the Yo-Yo Lifestyle of Chronic Dieting.* Thomas Nelson.

Being a Woman:

- Eldredge, John and Stasi. (2005). *Captivating. Unveiling The Mystery of a Woman's Soul.* Thomas Nelson.

- Franklin, Regina. (2004). *Who Calls Me Beautiful? Finding Our true Image in the Mirror of God.* Discovery House Publishers.

- Hagee, Diana. (2001). *The King's Daughter. Becoming the Woman God Created You to Be.* Thomas Nelson.

Emotional and Mental Healing:

- Evans, Jimmy. (2021). *21 Day Inner Healing Journey. A Personal Guide To Healing Past Hurts And Becoming Emotionally Healthier.* XO Publishing.

- Evans, Jimmy. (2022). *21 Day Total Freedom Journey. A Personal Guide To Finding Freedom For Your Heart, Mind, And Soul.* XO Publishing.

- Cloud, Dr. Henry and Townsend, Dr. John. (1992). *Boundaries. When To Say Yes, How To Say No To Take Control Of Your Life.* Zondervan.

- Arterburn, Stephen. (2005). *Healing Is A Choice. Ten Decisions That Will Transform Your Life & Ten Lies That Can Prevent You From Making Them.* Thomas Nelson.

- Fileta, Debra. (2023). *Reset. Powerful Habits To Own Your Thoughts, Understand Your Feelings & Change Your Life.* Harvest House Publishing.

- Terkeurst, Lysa. (2020). *Forgiving What You Can't Forget. Discover How To Move On, Make Peace With Painful Memories, And Create A Life That's Beautiful Again.* Nelson Books.

Life:

- Sadler, Julia Jeffress. (2019). *Pray Big Things. The Surprising Life God Has for You When You're Bold Enough To Ask.* BakerBooks.

Biblical Studies:

- Harris, Greg. (2008). *The Darkness and the Glory. His Cup and the Glory from Gethsemane to the Ascension.* Kress Christian Publications.

- Wright, Christopher J.H. (2014). *Knowing Jesus through the Old Testament. Second Edition.* IVP Academic.

- Harris, Greg. (2020). *The Bible Expositor's Handbook. Old & New Testaments.* B&H Academic.

- Harris, Greg. (2015). *The Stone And The Glory Of Israel. An Invi-*

tation For the Jewish People to Meet Their Messiah. Kress Biblical Resources.

Professional Help and Resources:

- **Suicide:**

- National suicide hotline https://988lifeline.org   Dial or text 988

- **Rape/Molestation:**

- https://www.rainn.org/resources   800-656-4673

- **Pregnancy:**

- Embrace Grace-https://embracegrace.comHeartbeat

- International https://www.heartbeatinternational.org/

- **Alcohol/Drug:**

- Celebrate Recovery-https://celebraterecovery.com

- Re:Generation Recovery-https://www.regenerationrecovery.org/

- **Porn:**

- Covenant Eyes-https://www.covenanteyes.com/

- **Counselors:**

- American Association of Christian Counselors-https://aacc.net/

- **Marriage Coaches:**

- Marriage In Motion: 365-https://www.marriageinmotion365.org

About the Author

Heidi Drury is a dedicated Christian marriage coach, holding three degrees: an Associate of Arts (AA), an Associate of Science (AS), and a Bachelor of Arts (BA). She has also pursued post-graduate work in education, emphasizing early childhood development and linguistics. She was certified as a marriage mediator at the XO Marriage Mediator Institute in October 2021, and is also trained to work with couples' attachment styles. With this specialized training, she brings a unique perspective to her coaching practice, empowering couples to navigate the complexities of married life with grace and wisdom. She has extensive experience working in women's ministry, marriage ministry, and addiction coaching, providing her with a well-rounded understanding of the challenges couples face in their relationships.

Heidi and her husband have been together for 18 years and share a blended family with 5 children and 7 grandchildren. Outside of her professional endeavors, Heidi finds joy in nature through exploring, hiking and traveling. She loves to embark on new adventures with her husband by discovering new destinations and different cultures and environments worldwide.

Above all, Heidi's greatest passion lies in sharing the profound impact of her faith journey. She aspires to continue sharing her transformative journey to inspire and equip others through future publications and speaking engagements. In Heidi's words, "Your past doesn't define you, God does. Your mistakes don't diminish you; God uses them for His glory. And your worth isn't contingent on others' approval-it is rooted in the unshakable love of a God who sees your beauty amidst your brokenness." She invites you to discover this same freedom and abundant life found in surrendering to the transformational power of your Father's love.

Your Journey to Healing & Redemption Continues Here

Thank you for joining me on this transformative journey through *From Thorns to Blossoms*. If my story has touched your heart and you're ready to take the next step toward healing and growth, I invite you to connect with me further.

Hire Us as Your Marriage Coaches

Are you struggling to resolve conflicts in your marriage? Do you long for deeper communication and a stronger connection with your spouse? Did you bring emotional baggage into your marriage that is affecting how you resolve conflict and communicate with your spouse? As Christian marriage coaches, we are her to guide you through the process of healing and transforming your relationship on a foundation of faith and love.

Visit Our Website

Discover more resources, articles and insights to help you navigate your own path to freedom. Our website offers information to support and inspire you on your journey.

Visit Us at www.marriageinmotion365.org

Stay Connected

Join our community on social media to receive daily inspiration, practical tips, and updates. Follow us on Facebook and Instagram for exclusive content and to be part of a supportive community.

<u>Follow Us on Facebook-</u> Marriage In Motion: 365

<u>Follow Us on Instagram</u> @marriageinmotion365

Email us hello@marriageinmotion365.org

Call us 903-836-2194

Embark on your journey of healing, redemption and the freedom found in God's love.

We look forward to walking alongside you.

In His Grace,

Heidi Drury